From the
Fields
to the
Garden
II

A second chapter in the life story of legendary cutman
Jacob "Stitch" Duran

Copyright © 2016 Jacob "Stitch" Duran, Zac Robinson
All rights reserved

Cover design by Oscar Avila
Interior design and formatting by BMP Digital

ISBN-13: 978-0-9984437-0-6
Zbooks llc

Jacob "Stitch" Duran
with Zac Robinson

CONTENTS

Foreword 1

PART 1: The Call 3
    1 Reminiscing 8
    2 A Changing of the Guard 12

PART 2: MMA 19
    3 Anderson Silva 20
    4 Cain Velasquez 24
    5 Shogun vs. Hendo 27
    6 The Knockouts 29
    7 Hero 33
    8 An Empty Seat 37
    9 Native 101 40
    10 Invicta FC 44

PART 3: Boxing 49
    11 Planes, Trains, and Automobiles Part One 54
    12 Planes, Trains, and Automobiles Part Two 57
    13 Royalty 60
    14 Planes, Trains, and Automobiles Part Three 62
    15 Andre Ward 65
    16 The Klitschkos 68

17 The Hyatt 72

PART 4: Behind the Scenes 75
18 Leon Tabbs 78
19 Burt Watson 82
20 Huitzi Mata 86
21 Emanuel Steward 91
22 Marc Ratner 94
23 The Cutmen 96

PART 5: Show Business 101
24 Here Comes the Boom 102
25 Creed 106
26 Rocky 111
27 Latin Legends 114
28 Giving Back 120

PART 6: Supporting the Troops 125
29 On the Way to Afghanistan 126
30 Down Range Gear 131
31 Bad Mofos 135
32 Killer 138
33 Explosion 142
34 Armed Forces Entertainment 145

PART 7: The Reebok Deal 151
35 The Middleman 152
36 Growth? 156
37 Fight Week 159
38 Support 162

PART 8: A New Beginning 167
39 WSOF and Bellator 168
40 Options 171
41 Rizin 174
42 Fighters First 178

43 Final Chapter 180

Meeting Stitch 183

Stitch's Top Lists 201

About the Authors 205

FOREWORD

Legends and legacies are formed and etched in stone by a body of work. Very few men achieve that status in a lifetime of commitment to doing the thing they love to do.

Stitch Duran is such a man. Untrained and untaught in a craft that calls for will and skill, Stitch Duran spent his time perfecting his craft to the point of becoming one of the best in the world and one of the best there ever was.

Over the past thirty years of my knowledge and working with Stitch, I've experienced his command of the craft as a cutman in some of the highest profile boxing and MMA events in the history of either sport. It was this perfection that caught the attention of some notable champions: The Klitschkos, Andre Ward, Randy Couture, Chuck Liddell, and a host of many others. Not only the fighters themselves, but many of their camp members, legendary promoters, and even some of the most prominent television executives at the major networks, have recognized Stitch's abilities. It was also those skills that caught the eye of Sylvester Stallone and took his art to the big screen.

The skills and knowledge of being a professional cutman in either sport from its early years to now, has always been a craft of

OJT (On-the-job training) and being self-taught. It took a special person and a special commitment for one to succeed.

The art of dressing a cut and stopping the bleeding of a fighter in the midst of what could be the fight of his life, the attention to detail, the ability to administer the wound in hope of stoppage so not to affect the outcome of the bout, is probably just as intense as the fight itself.

A good cutman is one part of the equation that has to be right, or everything else can go wrong.

Stitch is truly Da Man...

— Burt Watson

PART 1:

THE CALL

My shoulders still burned from the workout I'd done earlier in the morning with my son, Daniel. He was a great high school football player, and we love working out together. It used to be that he'd have to work to keep up with me. Now it's the other way around, and I'm steadily losing ground.

Charlotte and I like to shop at Costco when Daniel is working. He always takes a moment to greet us with a kiss and a smile before he darts off back to work. I pulled into a parking place and shut off the engine.

I opened my car door and the heat slapped me in the face. Vegas in July is scorching hot. Charlotte and I hurried through the stifling heat as it rose from the dark asphalt. Daniel saw us and popped over to give his mom a kiss on the cheek. "Tough workout this morning, Dad," he said to me.

"I know. I'm feeling it," I replied.

He hurried off back to his job and we walked inside. With the cool air we felt like we could catch our breaths again. As we were walking the aisles and loading our cart, my phone rang. It was Jess Gonzalez. The cutmen have always had a great relationship with Jess.

After two grueling days of fights in Brazil, with a UFC event the first night and the TUF show the next day, Jess gathered the cutmen, refs, and judges and told us what a great job we did.

With all the years that I worked in the UFC the only executives that gave us any praise were the guys from the UK, Marshall Zelaznik and Dave Lewis, and then Jess.

That five-minute meeting in Brazil was so powerful that it became the main topic between us cutmen and refs and judges at dinner that night.

I was worried about this phone call, and for good reason.

"Stitch, are you available to talk?" Jess asked.

"I'm at the store right now. I'll be home in an hour. Is that good?" I asked.

He said it was.

I hung up and we continued shopping as the weight of the impending call hung over my head.

I drove home with the AC blasting and my mind still spinning. I guessed that this call was about the interview I did about Reebok. The response from the fans was brutal to the UFC, Dana, and Reebok. It could go one of two ways. The UFC and Reebok recognized that they could make this into a positive and include the cutmen, or I was in deep shit.

Once home, I gave Charlotte the groceries and walked into my office. I sat in my chair, put my feet up on my desk, and waited.

It wasn't long before my phone rang. It was Jess Gonzalez and Marc Ratner, a UFC executive and a man I have a tremendous amount of respect for. Marc and I go way back to the days before the UFC when he was the top brass for the Nevada State Athletic Commission. He got right to the point. "Stitch, because of the interview you did about Reebok, the UFC is not going to use you anymore."

Those words hit me like a ton of bricks and sat on my chest.

There was a pause as the news sank in. I knew this was hard

for him also, and he was just the messenger. I didn't want to bust his balls. I breathed deeply. "I respect you, Marc. But do me a favor and tell Dana that he doesn't have any balls. He should have called me personally since he was the one who brought me in."

"I understand," he said.

We left it at that and hung up.

Charlotte had come into my office when the phone rang. I looked up at her as a rush of adrenaline coursed through my veins. "Crap, did that just happen? Did I really screw up?"

Charlotte crossed the room and placed her hand on my shoulder. She had been with me the whole time and knew this was a big moment. She has supported me all the way and been one of my pillars of strength. My mind was going a thousand miles per second. "Did that really just happen? After giving everything I had for the last fifteen years it was over just like that?"

"Well, it happened," she said, and then gave me a hug. "We'll be alright, and I'm proud of you for sticking to your values."

I nodded, but I was still in a little bit of shock.

She left to finish dinner, and I noticed that I just received a tweet, one of hundreds of the tweets and messages I'd been receiving from all over the world. It was from a supportive fan I'd never met named David Estrada. I replied with, "You will be the first to know that the UFC just let me go because I spoke out about the Reebok deal. Got to look for a new job!"

I've often wondered what David Estrada thought when he read my response, and if he recognized that it would change my life forever.

The tweet set off the firestorm. In a week I did fifty-seven interviews worldwide and actually had camera crews coming to my house.

I'll give you more details about all of this later. It was obviously a stunning and well-publicized moment in my life, and on the surface a pretty bad one, but it was just one moment that happened on July 22, 2015. Almost all of my experiences in the combat sports world have been overwhelmingly positive. I covered many of them in my first book, and when I left off it was during an incredible weekend that involved a trip back home and UFC 104 in Los Angeles.

As I left my hometown and the fields of Planada for the long drive to Los Angeles, I wrote that, "I was driving away from the world that knew me as Jacob Duran and driving into the one that knew me as Stitch."

A whole lot has happened between that moment in October 2009, and when I got the call that I had been released by the UFC for speaking the truth.

Let me start from the beginning and tell you all about it.

1 REMINISCING

As I settled into the five-hour drive from Planada to UFC 104 in Los Angeles, my mind began to wander. I spent the first part of my life working in the fields. As I often say to people, "If you can wear it or eat it, I've probably picked it."

It all started when I was just five years old. I lived with my mother, father, uncle, and six brothers and sisters in a tiny two-bedroom house on Hadley's camp.

My parents had their own room. The older kids, Dorothy, Jimmy, Benny, and Linda, shared the other room. My Uncle Miguel, and my brothers, Michael and Ernie, and then I, all slept in the living room. My youngest sister, Belen, was not born yet.

I dreamed of Disneyland while picking cotton with my mother, uncle, and brothers and sisters. My father was the foreman and made sure everyone got paid for the cotton they picked. We didn't have much in the way of material things, but we all supported each other. We recognized that we were in it together, and we didn't need that much to be happy.

My oldest sister, Dorothy, often reminisces about the time we lived in the camp. She once said, "Daddy always had meat on the table for us. We raised cows, pigs, rabbits, chickens, turkeys, and goats, and my tio (uncle) and Daddy would butcher the animals.

They became master butchers. Fruits and vegetables were plentiful," and then she smiled, "cakes, sodas and potato chips were a treat."

I eased onto the 99 heading south towards Los Angeles, and I thought about my friends, Chulo, Marcial, and Noe, who were by my side when we were little and still by my side to this day. There is a certain bond that people from Planada have. We are proud of the honest work we do and know that we have each other's back.

When my first book came out I was amazed with the outpouring of support from my old community. I was letting the world know that Planada existed. It was amazing and humbling.

As I passed through Chowchilla, I remembered the canal, Peter Deep. We had a lot of good times swimming there, and the corners of my mouth turned upward into a smile when I remembered the time Marcial and I lost our shoes to the rumbling water. It wasn't funny at all when it happened.

Then there was baseball. Man, I loved playing baseball, and I was pretty good. I had dreams of following in the footsteps of my hero, Roberto Clemente. A brief stint at Merced College was the end of my baseball career. I didn't have the money or transportation to stay.

Baseball of course reminded me of more of my friends. Great guys like Rudy Salcido, Jerry Zarate, and Alfred Sanchez, all lifelong friends.

It was by no means an easy upbringing. I spent a great amount of time working in the fields, even freezing mornings at around two or three when the farmers would call us to go smudge. Smudging was a process where we lined up hundreds of diesel cans (smudge pots) in the fields and lit them. The heat from the pots kept the young plants from freezing.

Because agriculture was a way of life for us in the San Joaquin Valley, the dozen or so high school kids that smudged the night before were excused from school the next day. Many of us would still go to school with smudge soot around our eyes, and our ears and nose and lungs filled with diesel smoke.

Smudging was eventually banned because of the heavy pollution it created by burning diesel. It wasn't very good for the kids who did it either.

Being naive, we did not understand the dangers that went with lighting the smudge pots at a young age. We did it because it was expected of us.

What my parents instilled was a sense of pride and a desire to work hard. My youth showed me how important it was to have those in your life who would support you and for you to support them as well.

When I joined the Air Force and moved to Thailand I received a different kind of support from my martial arts instructors. And then after the military I could not have done what I did without the support of my family.

I opened a gym called the American School of Kickboxing (ASK) in Fairfield. I didn't have the money, so I ran up a credit card debt just to get the doors open. Charlotte was there with me every step of the way.

Finally, the ultimate test of support was when I received the offer from my employer, RJ Reynolds, to move to Las Vegas. I'd wanted to pursue being a cutman and knew that Vegas was where I needed to be. The job came with a huge catch in the form of a $25,000 pay cut. And on top of that we only had a week to pack up and move.

Despite the difficulty and uncertainty, Charlotte and my kids, Carla, Jacob, Angela, and Daniel, were fully onboard. They've always been one hundred percent by my side throughout my career, during the good times and the bad.

With Bakersfield looming to the south as I made my way to UFC 104, I couldn't help but remember the drive to Las Vegas. We were packed up like the Beverly Hillbillies and stopped to stay the night in Bakersfield. A guy was murdered right outside of our hotel, and I wondered at the time if this was bad omen. It wasn't.

I'm so thankful for everyone I've had in my life. From my family and friends growing up, to my own family, and then there are all those who have supported my career through encouragement or sponsorship.

When I finally arrived at UFC 104, I felt energized and ready to go. I'd learned through the years that I'd better be ready for anything when it came to the fight game. I always prepare for the worst-case scenario because sometimes that's what happens.

I didn't know it at the time, but over the next half dozen years I'd experience a lot more unique and crazy things in combat sports.

2 A CHANGING OF THE GUARD

A subtle shift started happening in the UFC in 2010. I think a lot of things came together to make it happen, and it's not necessarily bad in all aspects. It's just part of the sport as it grows and changes. Beginning in 2010, a lot of the fighters that fans had loved during much of the 2000s began to retire.

In February, Frank Trigg fought for the last time, a loss to Matt Serra. Trigg had been involved in some of the greatest fights in the history of the sport. In September of the same year it was Serra's turn to hang them up after a loss to Chris Lytle.

I have two quick stories that come to mind with Frank and Matt. Once, Trigg had a shattered hand before a fight. He didn't tell anybody about it, and I wrapped his hands. I always asked the guys if they have any problems. He told me that he was good. I wrapped him and he went out and fought. It was only later that he revealed on MMAJunkie Radio that his hand was broken in multiple places. He'd said that if it weren't for my hand wrapping he never would have been able to fight.

Everybody remembers when Matt Serra shocked GSP to win the belt. Well, he considered me his good luck charm, and didn't want anybody else to wrap his hands. Burt Watson actually came out and pulled me from the cage to wrap Serra's hands, and he went on to win the belt.

In between the retirements of Trigg and Serra, Chuck Liddell fought for the last time. This one came at UFC 115 against Rich Franklin.

Chuck Liddell is the man that I never like to make eye contact with because he scares the crap out of me. That Mohawk. That stare. Those tattoos. Damn.

He was a larger-than-life fighter who thrilled us with his knockout power for many years. At 115, I was in his corner. He landed a kick that Rich blocked early on in the fight. We'd later find out that it actually broke Rich's arm. Yes, Rich Franklin is that much of a badass. He continued to fight Chuck Liddell with a broken arm. For most of the fight it looked like Chuck had Rich on his heels, but then he overcommitted with a big right hand. Rich countered with a right of his own.

Just like that, Chuck's long and illustrious career came to an end. I got to Chuck as fast as I could. He had a cut right in the middle of his top lip up to his nose. It looked like somebody had taken a knife and sliced it. I quickly put a towel on it and applied a bit of pressure. There was nothing I could really do for it, but I wanted the cut to be covered up as best as possible.

I did this out of respect to such a warrior. He'd lost, and disappointment was etched on his face. I didn't want the world to groan at the terrible gash on top of it. When he got his composure I told him to keep the towel so he could hold it to the cut. He did so, and to this day I don't think most people even recognized just how badly he was hurt.

He walked away with the towel I gave him still pressed to his mouth, and it would be the last time he fought. This is a man who first entered the Octagon at UFC 17 in 1998. He was there in the earlier days and was a huge part of ushering the sport along through much of the 2000s. With his Mohawk and tattoos he still might be the most recognizable fighter of all time.

Despite me saying I was scared to look into Chuck's eyes, he really wasn't an animal by any stretch. On a few occasions after working his corner I got a call from his coach, John Hackleman, to tell me how much he and Chuck appreciated me being there for them. Moments like that are priceless to me.

This was just the beginning of the end when it came to UFC legends. I started to say pioneers, and in some regards these guys were. But many of them came along during the dark ages and then blossomed as the UFC changed and regained popularity. I have to give Dana White and Lorenzo and Frank Fertitta a lot of credit for that. They did a wonderful job building a platform for these amazing fighters, and once in the spotlight they put on amazing fights.

Less than a year after Chuck Liddell retired, one of his biggest rivals also fought for the last time. Randy Couture is probably one of the nicest guys I've ever met. He always had me smiling every time I wrapped his hands. I'd sit across from him, his hand on the back of a chair, and work to form the only piece of equipment he'd take into the cage with him. He was always relaxed and joking around. I believe one of my most important jobs is helping to calm the fighter as I wrap their hands. I watch them and listen to them to determine how I can give them that little extra that will help prepare them before combat.

With Randy, it was almost the opposite. It was like sitting down to have lunch with an old friend. But then, once they put that pin in the cage door that lunchtime easy-going Randy disappeared. He became what we all saw, a tremendous competitor and champion.

In April 2011, at UFC 129 in front of over 55,000 people, we saw Randy fight for the last time. Sadly, he too ended by getting knocked out when Lyoto Machida threw an amazing flying front kick. He gave us fourteen incredible years inside the cage, and I'm honored to have gotten to work with him.

Really, it's an honor to work with all of these guys. We're talking some bad dudes, some of the baddest on the planet, and through my job as a cutman I got to play a small role in their careers.

It was only a handful of months later when another former champion, Matt Hughes, fought for the last time. Matt is the one who hooked me up with Mark Zacher, the owner of One More Round, an apparel company that many fans thought I owned. Mark sponsored Matt, and Matt told him, "If anyone gives the fighters one more round, it's Stitch."

The rest is history, and fans still yell out, "One more round!" to me at events.

Think about that. In a span of a little over a year Chuck Liddell, Randy Couture, and Matt Hughes fought for the last time. It didn't end there. In July 2012, Forrest Griffin fought Tito Ortiz at UFC 148. The two warriors earned fight of the night honors, and it would be Griffin's last time in the cage.

Forrest will always have a special place in my heart. I was able to keep him in the fight a time or two. The first, and most well publicized, was during the TUF finale when he and Stephan Bonnar skyrocketed the sport with their slugfest. Forrest got cut badly, and I worked to keep him in the fight. And of course we know what happened after that. The UFC and MMA became a sport that was on the map of the mainstream.

And then there was UFC 76 when he fought Shogun Rua. Forrest got a nasty lightning bolt cut on his forehead. I did some of my best work ever on that cut. My first book actually opens with this story. The cut didn't bleed during the third round when Forrest sunk in the rear naked choke. That victory was named upset of the year in 2007.

Forrest showed his appreciation by sending me a gift certificate to a really nice restaurant. It just showed up in the mail one day. He took the time to think of me and send it. It was such an honor to receive it. Forrest is a class act. He's also a hilarious guy. If you've read his books you know that.

One time after wrapping his hands he raised his fists and that skewed smile appeared on his face. "Man, these feel so good I could punch my mother!" he said with a laugh.

The whole dressing room cracked up. I couldn't help but laugh as well.

Finally, there was Georges St. Pierre. I see him as something of a bridge between the earlier years of the sport to today's version. He is such an all-around fighter with amazing skill and work ethic. It was on the UFC's 20th anniversary at UFC 167 in November 2013, when GSP fought Johny Hendricks. It was an absolute bloodbath, and it appeared that GSP had taken the brunt of the beating. But he earned the split decision victory.

Afterward, he vacated the belt.

GSP's fight happened only a few months after the deal with Fox was announced. This was a huge step forward for the sport. But in a way that I can't really explain, it also kind of created a little shift that began to distance some of the earlier fans. Maybe it's because the UFC did such a good job of building up a format that worked so well during the 2000s. The sport was on the fringes of the mainstream with millions of fans all over the world. It was doing great on Spike and fans connected with the fighters like no other sport. And then it began to change when we saw these incredible fighters from the 2000s retire at about the same time the UFC took massive steps toward the mainstream with Fox.

I can't blame the UFC for this. When it comes to business they built a profitable company by forming these big deals. I think it had the unintended effect of creating a gap that separated the old golden age from the new edition. The fighters who entered the UFC during the transition period gave us some great fights, and the skill level was improving as MMA gained popularity worldwide. Believe me, I'm not knocking the current fighters in any way. They are amazing athletes and competitors.

I guess it can be equated to throwing a rock in a pond. When it first splashes into the water there are a few big ripples. As more and more ripples appear those old ones spread and fade. I loved my time with the UFC during those years, and I'm glad they had the foresight to bring me in to help out Leon Tabbs way back in 2001. Dan Hardy might have said it best when he learned that I was out of the UFC. He tweeted, "So sad to hear that Stitch Duran will no longer be around during fight week. It's the end of an era. The golden age of MMA has passed."

I'm fully aware that I played a small role in that golden age. It was an important role, but it was the guys I mentioned above who really made it happen. It was those guys we all loved watching, and it was them who made the sport great.

It still is great, just different. And I have a ton of respect and some great stories with the fighters from this new age as well.

PART 2:

MMA

3 ANDERSON SILVA

On February 6, 2010, Chael Sonnen fought Nate Marquardt at UFC 109 in a middleweight title eliminator. Aside from nearly being KO'd with a knee and almost being submitted with a Guillotine, Sonnen dominated the fight and scored the unanimous decision. As soon as the fight was over, the shit storm began. Really, it had been brewing for some time because Sonnen had directed much of his talk at Anderson.

Somewhere around 2008 or 2009, it was like a flip switched with Sonnen. He went from being a normal very good fighter to being a smack-talking king, and he backed up all that talk with wins in the cage.

When Sonnen beat Marquardt, Anderson Silva was nearly four years into his incredible run as the middleweight champ. Silva was scheduled to fight Vitor Belfort at the time, and when asked about whom he'd rather face, Sonnen said, "I hope Anderson wins because I think Vitor's a lot tougher fighter. If I had to choose between the two, I'm going to take the low road and take the easier opponent to get to the championship."

Belfort got hurt. Silva ended up fighting Demian Maia in Abu Dhabi in front of the royal family in April 2010, and it was one of the strangest fights ever. Maia couldn't do anything to Silva, and

Silva seemed bored on his way to the decision victory.

This set up UFC 117. Anderson and Chael would finally fight, and it was in my old stomping grounds of Oakland. I'd worked there for years as I pursued my dream of being a cutman. I'd honed my boxing skills at the famous King's gym and still have a lot of great friends in Oakland.

Before the fight, Chael said, "I became the number one contender on February 6, and on February 7 he put out a press release on why he shouldn't have to fight me…"

He also said, "I'm here purely to win the world championship, period. It doesn't have a lot to do with Anderson. Getting to beat up Anderson is just a bonus."

These quotes were just a couple in a long line of scathing comments directed at Anderson. I've had a long relationship with Anderson and I love that guy. When I went in to wrap his hands before UFC 117, I was really interested to see how the buildup and Chael's comments had affected him.

He was his normal friendly self, but there was a little bit more intensity and focus than I'd seen before. I remember thinking, like many others, that there was a very good chance he was going to absolutely maul Chael.

As we all soon found out, that wasn't the case. The fight started, and Chael was all over Anderson. He took him down and beat him up like nobody had ever done before. Anderson's manager, Ed Soares, was sitting next to me, and we watched as Anderson was taking a barrage of punches and getting the shit beat out of him.

It was really shocking to be sitting five steps from the cage as it unfolded. Normally, as a cutman I don't go into the cage until I see swelling or a cut, but in this situation I decided that I needed to do some preventative maintenance, especially with this being a five rounder.

"I'm going to go in at the first round," I told Ed.

When the bell sounded, I hustled through the cage door and did what I could to keep Anderson's beaten face from swelling too much. And in the second round, and then the third, he continued to get pummeled. I think it was after the third round when he was talking about his ribs. I was too busy focusing on the swelling on his face to consider doing anything to help his ribs.

Ed didn't say much to me throughout the fight, but it was obvious that his concern had continued to grow. We were watching the belt change hands in incredible fashion.

Silva hung in the fight despite taking a massive beating, and then it happened. With less than two minutes left he slapped a triangle on Sonnen and transitioned to an armbar. Chael tapped. Silva retained his belt.

It was a chaotic and incredible fight. Chael Sonnen had talked all kinds of shit, and then he backed it up until the very end. I'd done everything I could during that fight to keep Anderson in it, and being the champion that he is, he pulled off the miracle.

It was almost three weeks after that fight when I was in a taxi after the long flight across the United States. I was in Boston for the UFC's first ever event in Massachusetts. The event had a fan expo beforehand, and there were people everywhere as the taxi pulled up to drop me off at the hotel.

I climbed out and noticed a group of probably twenty or so fans surrounding Anderson Silva. He was taking pictures and signing autographs. He told them to hold on and he'd be back, and then hurried over to where I was.

He came up to me and gave me a big hug. "Thank you," he said.

He didn't say anything else, just thank you. It was a powerful moment knowing what had transpired in that fight where I kept him in it and he eventually won. I knew exactly how much those two words meant. And he knew how much they meant.

He gave me a smile and a nod and hustled back over to the

waiting fans. In a matter of moments fans surrounded me as well. I was already excited to be in Boston for the first time, and those two words made it that much better.

So often in the cutman business it's the little things like this that have so much meaning. We form bonds with the fighters, and it means the world when they show their appreciation for what we do.

4 CAIN VELASQUEZ

American Kickboxing Academy in San Jose is well known as one of the best MMA gyms in the world. Javier Mendez founded it back in the late '90s. His first big-name fighter was Frank Shamrock. His next was BJ Penn. Because of this huge success in the early years of MMA, that is where Javier has gained his notoriety.

I knew Javier Mendez even before his MMA days. We were involved in the kickboxing world around the same time. He was an ISKA champion and trained many champion kickboxers.

I'm guessing it was in 2007 when Javier and I were talking at an event. "I've got this Mexican heavyweight who's going to be a world champion."

It seems that almost on a weekly basis somebody will tell me that they have somebody or know somebody, or even are somebody who will become a champion. I wish them the best while thinking that it isn't going to happen.

Javier Mendez isn't just anybody, so his assertion held a little more weight, but a Mexican heavyweight champion? He had to be reaching.

It wasn't long after that when I wrapped Cain Velasquez for the first time. He was a quiet and serious guy. And then he got in the cage and mauled Brad Morris. He then went on to destroy one guy after another, and Javier's words drifted through my head every time Cain's hands were raised in victory.

Finally, it was his time at UFC 121. Cain was taking on the larger-than-life destroyer, Brock Lesnar.

I wrapped both Cain and Brock at UFC 121 in Anaheim. When Brock first came into the UFC he wanted a test run with me wrapping his hands. It was UFC 81 and I had my daughter, Carla, with me. She's a huge WWE fan and was excited to meet Brock. He loved the wraps, and then I cut them off and he signed them for Carla. Since then, I'd always wrapped Brock's hands.

The energy in the Honda Center when Brock and Cain met in the center of the cage was electric. The hairs on my arms stood. I was in Brock's corner, and I watched as he rushed toward Cain at the start of the fight. He couldn't get Cain down, and when he finally did take him down, Cain popped right back up.

Cain was like a machine. He landed shot after shot on Brock and kept coming like the Terminator. Brock did everything he could, but late in the first round he was turtled up and Cain was delivering brutal hammer fists.

He was cut badly on the left side of his face, and with less than a minute left in round one, Herb Dean jumped in to stop the fight.

I rushed over to Brock to take care of him. I applied the swab to the cut and it sank all the way to the bone. I removed the swab and applied pressure with my fingers to close up the cut. As soon as I let it go, it opened right back up.

As I was working on the cut, Brock said, "Stitch, take care of me."

"Absolutely," I replied.

Brock is as big and bad as they come, and through his time in the UFC we developed a real mutual respect. I'd even say we'd become friends. Before one of his fights somebody told me that Brock had a shirt for me. As we all know, he's a pretty intense guy.

As I was pulling on his 4XL gloves I said, "Brock, did you really pack a shirt for me?"

He smiled. "Yes, my wife asked if she should pack one for Stitch, and I told her yes."

He went on to tell me that I was part of the team.

It was a unique experience. I was glad to be there for him, while at the same time I felt terrible for what he was going through. On the other side of the coin, I understood how ecstatic Cain Velasquez and Javier Mendez were at that moment, and I was happy for them.

As I was packing up my stuff in the dressing room I saw that the doctors were stitching Brock up. I knew he was in good hands and slipped out the door.

Not long after that fight I saw Javier. I brought up what he'd said way back in 2007 about Cain becoming a champion. "You know how many times I've heard that?" I asked Javier. "Especially being a Mexican heavyweight. But lo and behold, he became a champion."

I guess the moral of the story is that you should never doubt Javier Mendez, and there are times when even the toughest men in the world need support.

5 SHOGUN VS. HENDO

Bernard Hopkins had 66 professional fights and spent 506 rounds inside the ring. He was forty-eight years old for his last fight in 2014. In my mind, Dan Henderson is the Bernard Hopkins of MMA. He's a mature and sharp fighter, and he's always dangerous.

My experience with both Shogun Rua and Hendo goes way back to the old PRIDE days. As a matter of fact, it was Shogun and Wanderlei Silva who gave me the nickname Santana. Now, pretty much every time I see the older Brazilian fighters they greet me with an emphatic, "Santana!"

For the longest time Rua always asked when I was going to wrap his hands. I replied with, "Soon."

The first time I wrapped his hands was in the rematch against Lyoto Machida when he scored a knock out to claim the light heavyweight belt.

I wrapped Shogun's hands before his fight with Hendo at UFC 139 as well, and I was in his corner.

Everybody knew going in that both fighters were explosive and dangerous. We all expected a good fight, but I don't think anybody could have expected what we got.

Hendo and Shogun went toe-to-toe and gave us what would

later become the fight of the year for 2011. It was just two weeks before at UFC 138, Mark Munoz vs. Chris Leben in Birmingham, England, when the UFC implemented five rounds for non-title fights. That fight was stopped after the second round with Munoz scoring the TKO. The five-round rule couldn't have come at a better time with the show that Hendo and Shogun put on, at least sort of.

I say sort of because they just beat the hell out of each other, and I was in the cage between each round to work on Shogun. After the third round I met a swollen, bloody, and exhausted Rua in the middle of the cage and guided him to his corner so I could work on him. "That's the last round?" he asked me.

"Yeah, that's it," I replied.

I was working on him and the timekeeper gave the ten-second count. I thought, "Oh shit, he has two more rounds!"

Shogun was exhausted, and he trudged back out there to meet an equally exhausted Hendo. They continued to throw down trading shot after shot. To this day I don't know what gave Shogun the energy to continue for those two rounds, but he did.

It was an ultimate display of heart and guts and warrior spirit. Shogun lost the decision to Hendo, and I felt horrible for my mistake. When I saw Shogun later, I said, "I'm really sorry. I didn't know."

He shrugged it off. "It's okay," he replied.

Even though he forgave me for the screw up, I still felt bad about it. I wasn't used to the five-round non-title fights, but I should have remembered.

I try very hard to do everything right. The men and ladies in the cage deserve my best. Sometimes though, we all make mistakes. But what a great fight! The fans loved it. I loved it. Everybody loved it. And thankfully Shogun still calls me Santana.

6 THE KNOCKOUTS

Anderson Silva pretended to wobble after a soft left from Chris Weidman. Weidman landed another soft left, and then he missed with a big right and tossed his right hand out again, and missed. He didn't miss with the next left. It wasn't exactly a hard punch, but it caught Anderson right on the chin.

It was like he fell backwards in slow motion, arms and legs splayed out, and all hell broke loose in the MGM at UFC 162.

Rewind to a few hours before that. I wrapped both Silva's hands and Weidman's hands. Weidman has called me his go-to guy for hand wrapping, and he's an outstanding fighter and person. He was so focused and ready for the biggest fight of his life.

Silva was focused too, but much more relaxed. His team was wearing some really nice sweats. I commented on how much I liked them.

"I'll make sure to send you some," Anderson said.

As I was finishing wrapping hands, a member of the UFC staff stuck his head in. "Stitch, Edward James Olmos wants to meet you."

I was really excited about this. Olmos is one of my favorite actors, and you have no idea how many times I've been called Edward James Olmos. Even more than I've been called Geraldo.

There's a green screen backstage where they take photos of the fighters during the events. That's where EJO was waiting. I hustled toward it, excited to finally meet him. He was there because Anderson Silva was in a movie with him called *Monday Nights at Seven*. It's not exactly an MMA movie, more of a love story that was directed by Marty Sader, who was also at the event and had a fight scheduled that was actually going to be part of the movie. Sader gained fame for his role in *Most High*. He's a high-energy guy and big into MMA. He'd even been training for a few years.

As I approached the green screen, I saw EJO standing there with his arms folded. "Man, we do look alike!" I said with a laugh.

He laughed as well, and said that people in the audience kept calling him Stitch.

We started talking and were really having a good time. I began to tell him about my history. "You know I grew up as a farm worker in the central valley and wanted to play baseball—"

He held up his hands to stop me. "No, no, I know your whole story, Stitch."

I was pretty dumbfounded and humbled by that.

We talked a little more, and I said, "Listen, my mother is a huge fan. Would you mind talking to her?"

"I'd be happy to."

I got her on the phone and told her who I was with. He took the phone and said a lot of nice things about me, and man it was surreal to be standing there listening to EJO talking to my mother.

They were finishing up and he said. "We're going to get Stitch in the movie."

"Alright, well when you finish the movie I want you to come to the house and I'll make you some menudo and enchiladas," my mother said.

"That would be great," he replied.

It was an amazing experience for my mother and me.

Now, back to Anderson Silva. He fell to the canvas after that left hand. Weidman pounced. In a matter of seconds it was all over.

I rushed into the cage to take care of Anderson. As I got to him he was confused. He looked up at me as if to ask what happened. "You got knocked out," I said.

I never mince words when it comes to this moment. The fighters often don't know what happened. I want to be as clear and concise as I can so they can start to comprehend.

As my words registered, all the energy just drained from Anderson's body. He'd won the UFC middleweight belt almost six years earlier, and he'd never been knocked out. At that moment he realized that it was over.

He was in shock. Everybody was in shock. The MGM was in complete pandemonium.

As Anderson left the cage I saw him stop where Edward James Olmos, Marty Sader, and his wife and co-writer Laura Keys were sitting only a few rows from the cage. He hugged EJO and Laura, and then hugged Marty. I saw that Marty, who is a good friend of Anderson's, had tears in his eyes.

Later on, Marty said that in that terrible moment it was Anderson who was comforting and reassuring him by saying that everything would be okay and it was fine.

It was such an unreal night. I met Edward James Olmos and he talked to my mother, and then we all watched Chris Weidman shock the world by KO'ing Anderson.

A couple years later I was backstage at Resurrection Fighting Alliance 31 in downtown Las Vegas. Marty Sader was about to step into the cage against Corey Turner, and the cameras would be rolling for the movie. Totally unscripted, whatever happens, happens.

His fight was scheduled for the middle of the card so there would be more fans in the crowd. Unfortunately, the athletic commission changed it to the first fight with very little notice.

The cameras rolled and I wrapped Marty's hands. Anderson gave him last-minute instructions while EJO looked on.

Marty warmed up as quickly as he could, and then it was time to go. We walked toward the cage. "Keep your composure," I said. "This is a new experience."

I was in Marty's corner and ready to go. The fight started, and I looked down to adjust my bag. There was a crack. I looked up. Marty had been knocked out. I rushed into the cage to take care of him. His nose was broken and bleeding profusely. As I worked on him I was thinking that Marty is a real stud. He took one for the movie.

Marty is a guy who had trained for this. He wasn't just some actor who jumped into the cage unprepared. But—as we witnessed that night, and on so many other nights—anything can happen in a fight. Chris Weidman knocking out Anderson Silva is the ultimate confirmation of the cliché.

Once Marty was cleaned up, he went to the hospital for evaluation. EJO and I were still at the event and decided to grab a hotdog. The fans went crazy when they saw us. A crowd gathered around and we took pictures and talked with them for a long time as they were freaking out about how much we looked alike.

It was a good end to a night that was kind of a bummer.

In any event, check out *Monday Nights at Seven*. It's a unique and great movie. You'll see Anderson Silva, and my doppelganger, and now friend, is of course tremendous in it. You might even catch a glimpse of me.

As I drove home after RFA 31 I was buzzing with excitement about being in the movie, but even more so about working with Edward James Olmos.

Definitely one to scratch off my bucket list!

7 HERO

Fort Campbell sits right on the Kentucky/Tennessee border and got its start at almost the exact same time the Japanese bombed Pearl Harbor. It was originally a wartime training camp, but became a permanent installation not long after being built.

There was a tornado there not too long ago.

It is the home of the Screaming Eagles and the 5th Special Forces Group.

The Screaming Eagles parachute team pre-dates the Golden Knights.

And in 2005, a Private once opened fire on a group of soldiers at Fort Campbell. Fortunately, nobody was killed.

Now don't get me wrong. I'm not some kind of war history buff. I learned all this when I had the honor to work at Fort Campbell for Fight for the Troops 3.

This event happened a couple weeks after I'd returned from a life-changing trip to visit troops in Afghanistan, and I was really excited to be a part of it.

The main event was a fight between All-American badass, Tim Kennedy, and Rafael Natal. Other service members on the card included Liz Carmouche, a Marine with three tours to the

Middle East, and a Ranger, Colton Smith.

As I was wrapping hands backstage, I heard a voice say, "Stitch Duran!"

I looked in that direction to see General McConnell. He hosted us in Afghanistan a few weeks before. I hopped up and we gave each other a bear hug as the soldiers around him were probably thinking, who in the hell is this guy?

"What are you doing here?" I asked.

He joked. "I came here to see you."

Tim Kennedy was the last guy I wrapped. I knew he was in the military, but as I was backstage wrapping his hands I didn't realize just how bad of a dude he was. He smiled easy, but was serious heading into his main-event fight. At the time I had no idea that less than a year later I'd be in Europe with Tim on an American Forces Entertainment tour where I'd get to know him much better.

Unfortunately for all the military members dressed in their customary BDUs, both Liz Carmouche and Colton Smith lost their fights.

As I was sitting cageside at this event I couldn't help but remember my first Fight for the Troops back in 2008. At that one a soldier asked if I'd take a picture with him.

"Of course," I said.

And then he held up his prosthetic leg and asked me if I'd hold it. Chills ran through me thinking about what he'd been through. I instantly had to man up and held his leg and smiled for the picture. I think maybe they were messing with me to see what I'd do! But it also made me consider how well he'd adjusted to life after a terrible injury.

The other thing that I couldn't help but remember from my first Fight for the Troops was Corey Hill. He was a lanky 6'4" lightweight that became well known from *The Ultimate Fighter* season 5. At the first Fight for the Troops he suffered a terrible leg break when Dale Hartt checked his kick. I was right there with him during that awful injury.

I remember how he looked up at me and how I told him I'd take care of him. In that moment there was so much pain on his face, both physical and mental. All those hopes and dreams and desires that we all carry were in serious jeopardy of being ripped away from him in one instant.

As Corey was being wheeled out of the Octagon, his final words to me were, "I almost had him, Stitch."

Corey showed such a warrior spirit to recover from that injury, actually get back in the cage, and win.

As I sat there in Fort Campbell, Kentucky I thought of him and all the others who had been through so much, and yet they keep on going even when all the odds are stacked up against them like a brick wall. They lower their heads and run through it. These kids inspire me all the time.

Tragically, only a year and a half after I was thinking about Corey Hill and his leg break, I learned that he passed away from pneumonia and a collapsed lung. He was only thirty-six years old. All too often life isn't fair.

I was roused from those thoughts as Tim Kennedy made his way to the cage. The roar from the soldiers was deafening.

Bruce Buffer did his thing with class and pizzazz, as always, and then he introduced Rafael Natal. The hangar was eerily quiet as Bruce yelled out, "Rafael Natal!"

Then he introduced Tim Kennedy, and the roof almost came off.

Less than a minute into the fight a boisterous, "Ranger Up, Ranger Up," chant started.

Natal landed a leg kick to end the chant.

The two went back and forth, picking and choosing their shots for the next couple minutes. Rafael Natal looked pretty good, but then with twenty seconds left in round one Kennedy landed a big left. Just like that, the fight was over.

In the post-fight interview, Joe Rogan asked Tim how he was feeling. Talking to the crowd he said, "I love you guys so much…you guys are my heroes…"

This is coming from a guy who many people call a hero, and as I heard him say this I considered what makes someone a hero. Is it somebody who fights on even when they shouldn't be able to? Is it somebody who inspires others to achieve more? Is it somebody who deals with terrible adversity with teeth gritted and a smile on their face? Is it somebody who is willing to embrace the day-to-day grind and continue to plod along with no end in sight?

Then I decided that it was all of the above.

Damn, I love my job. But less than two months later I had a moment where I didn't love it so much.

8 AN EMPTY SEAT

In the MGM's dressing room at UFC 168 I saw Ronda Rousey before her rematch with Miesha Tate. She smiled and gave me a hug and a peck on the cheek.

A couple hours later I waited at the prep point to apply the Vaseline and tapped Don House on the arm. "Look at the way she looks and walks. She could be Chucky's little sister," I said with a chuckle.

It's amazing to me how she can go from being how she is backstage to being so incredibly intense as she makes her way to the cage. She's truly an ultimate competitor.

The rematch did not disappoint. Ronda and Miesha went at it for the first two rounds. Ronda was winning the fight and beating Tate up pretty good, but Tate was so tough and hung in the fight until the third round when Ronda finally locked in her patented armbar.

A side-note that I find interesting, that fight lasted almost eleven minutes. Ronda's first seven fights combined lasted just over twelve minutes!

The Ronda/Miesha fight was right after Josh Barnett lost to Travis Browne via brutal elbows. Josh has been a friend for a long time. He even took me over to Japan to be his cutman for PRIDE during the early 2000s. I'd also taught him how I wrap hands and he had become extremely proficient at it. I hated seeing him lose like he did.

The main event was the rematch between Anderson Silva and Chris Weidman. It was only six months earlier when Weidman knocked out Anderson to claim the belt. Some thought that Weidman would beat Anderson once again. Others thought that Anderson would fight like a man possessed and reclaim his belt. Nobody expected the fight would end like it did.

Once again, I wrapped both their hands. Weidman's demeanor was similar to how it was six months earlier. Anderson, on the other hand, was more focused and serious than usual.

Weidman rocked Anderson in the first round and looked really good. It seemed that maybe Anderson had finally met somebody who had his number. And then it happened.

Way back in October 1951, Bobby Thomson of the New York Giants hit a home run off of Ralph Branca to win the pennant. That home run became known as "The Shot Heard Round the World."

At UFC 168, Anderson Silva threw a kick that Chris Weidman checked, and it was the "Break Heard Round the World."

The snapping sound, like a tree branch breaking, is burned into my ears. As soon as I heard it, Corey Hill once again flashed through my mind. I knew that Anderson had broken his leg, and even before his foot started flopping in the air I was heading for the cage.

I got there with an ice pack in hand. Anderson was writhing on the canvas holding his left leg. The doctors were working on him, and I stood there numbly. There was nothing I could do. I watched as Herb Dean got a stool and started to help Anderson to it before realizing the severity of the injury, and I watched as the doctor tried to stabilize the leg.

I walked over to Chris and wiped him down. It's very seldom when I feel helpless in the cage. At that moment I did. I couldn't help Anderson in any way, and it was terrible.

At the start of the post-fight press conference there was an empty seat to Dana White's right where Anderson would have been sitting, win or lose. Instead, he was on his way to surgery. Kevin Iole, a great writer and friend from Yahoo Sports, asked Dana about Anderson.

"It's just one of those crazy things," Dana replied. "Never in a million years, you don't ever expect to see that…Anderson Silva's been amazing. He's one of the greatest of all time if not the best ever. It's a shitty way to see him go out, but it is part of the game."

Dana wasn't kidding. Even though I'd been through a similar leg break with Corey Hill, I never could have expected it to happen to Anderson at UFC 168. I almost never get bummed out about a fight ending, but this one got to me. Normally after an event I'm buzzing with energy and it takes a while to come down. Not this one.

I'd known Anderson for so long, and at that moment I really thought that his career was over. I went home and just sat around for about three hours. I fell asleep that night with images of Anderson on the canvas and me unable to help.

It sucked.

9 NATIVE 101

The waitress put the plate down and nodded as if proud to be serving it to me.

"Gracias," I said.

"De nada."

The escamoles was thick and looked like some kind of a bean or really large rice.

Huitzi Mata had just ordered the delicacy for me. For those who are really into MMA, they know Huitzi for his work as a cutman. He was an Aztec and a shaman who gave me many unique experiences towards the end of his life. I'll talk much more about him later.

The thought of actually not eating the escamoles flashed through my mind for the briefest of moments. You see, escamol is ant eggs or larvae. It comes from a large black ant that is very aggressive and venomous. Getting the eggs is dangerous and often painful work.

Not eating the eggs wasn't really an option. There was no way I could offend Huitzi and his master shaman. They had just taken me up the pyramids of Teotihuacan, an ancient city to the northeast of what is now Mexico City.

As we arrived at the base of the pyramid, we saw UFC fighter

Frank Trevino and his team absorbing the ancient history of the Aztec culture. Frank was fighting on the Mexico City card and this was his way of mentally preparing himself. Huitzi and his shaman invited them to join us.

Photo: Teotihuacan

It was an amazing journey up to the top of the pyramids. We followed Huitzi and his master as we traveled up the steps in a snake-like pattern in order to get the most out of the experience. It took us a long time to get to the top. By the time we reached it, my hair had become wet underneath my straw hat and sweat trickled down my brow.

We stood there enjoying the view as Huitzi's master talked of the Aztec culture and the importance of this place. The information added to the moment, and then we saw butterflies. "This is very good," Huitzi's master said. "It represents transformation to see butterflies, especially here."

The journey up the pyramid had left us hungry, so here I sat staring down at the heaping pile of ant eggs on my plate. Like I said, the thought of not eating the eggs was fleeting. I'm the type of guy that if I'm in someone else's culture I want to really experience it. I'd been all over the world and tried an unbelievable variety of foods. Escamoles would soon be added to my list.

I shoveled it into my mouth. It was soft to the bite, a consistency similar to cottage cheese. It had a buttery, kind of nutty flavor, and all in all it was pretty good, especially once I got over the fact that I was eating ant eggs and larvae.

Huitzi and his master were proud to have me try the delicacy, and I was honored that they had so willingly shared their Aztec culture with me.

I was in Mexico City for UFC 188. Cain Velasquez was finally defending his title against Fabricio Werdum. Back at UFC 180, some eight months earlier, Werdum had beaten Mark Hunt in the first ever event in Mexico. He'd become very popular after that win because he speaks beautiful Spanish and spent a lot of time there prior to the fight. And then when he got in the cage he stopped Hunt with a flying knee and punches.

I was able to go native 101 because I arrived for UFC 188 on Wednesday. Normally I get to events the day before. Huitzi was kind enough to let me stay with his family and then showed me around.

Mexico City was absolutely buzzing with excitement for the heavyweight title fight. Cain Velasquez had been on the shelf for almost two years due to injury. During that time, Fabricio Werdum had won the interim belt.

This set up the fight in Mexico City. As I mentioned earlier, Werdum had become really popular thanks to his first fight, and then he'd arrived in Mexico City almost two months before UFC 188 in order to train there and acclimate to the city's altitude of over 7,000 feet.

Of course Cain Velasquez, the first ever Mexican-American heavyweight champion, had a huge following too. Despite

Werdum's popularity, it was Cain who got the most attention going into 188, but he'd arrived just two weeks before the fight.

Cain is a pretty stoic guy. Every time I wrap his hands I make sure he gives me a smile and a hug. It's just a way that I think helps to prepare him. When I entered the dressing room to wrap him before 188, he seemed to be a little on the nervous side. It made sense considering it was such a big fight and he was coming off a long layoff, but he had a much harder time giving me the smile and hug.

The fight started under a pumped up crowed 21,000. Fabricio Werdum rocked Cain early and took control. He rocked Cain with heavy shot after heavy shot. As round one came to an end I hurried into the cage to work on Cain.

He was discombobulated and standing. I tried to work on him but he was moving his head around.

"Cain, let me work on you, let me work on you," I yelled to him.

There was no doubt that he was in very bad shape. He was gasping for air and seemed totally out of it. He went back out for round two, and Werdum continued to land big shots. Cain fought on despite the onslaught. It blows me away how sometimes these guys fight on when there is no way they should be able to. It's like they're able to reach so deep down inside of them to find every little bit of fight they have.

Round two came to an end and it was more of the same. I worked on Cain and he didn't seem to be all there. He was in serious trouble.

Finally, in round three Werdum was able to finish the fight with a guillotine choke to become the undisputed heavyweight champ. It was a well-deserved and impressive victory.

Afterward, I was talking with Dr. Davidson, a doctor for the UFC. He'd said that it seemed Cain was suffering from altitude sickness. It can cause people to become delusional, and it seemed to me that this is what happened to Cain.

I'm not taking anything away from Fabricio, and I know that Cain would not use this as an excuse, but it was like he was fighting with a plastic bag over his head.

Later on, when I ran into Cain again, he apologized. "I'm sorry, I just didn't know what was going on."

"It's okay," I replied. "I understand."

He of course didn't need to apologize to me. He was in a serious situation and wasn't able to think clearly.

Despite it being such a tough loss for Cain, it was an incredible few days for me. And with the untimely passing of Huitzi Mata, it makes it that much more special.

10 INVICTA FC

Back in early 2012, Shannon Knapp called to ask if I could help get cutmen for her new all-female promotion, Invicta FC. Ray Sefo had contacted me as well when he started the World Series of Fighting. I was happy to help both of them find cutmen. They are terrific people.

I was in Kansas City for Invicta 4. This was the promotion's first online pay-per-view event. Carla Esparza and Bec Hyatt were fighting for the inaugural strawweight title. I was working in Bec's corner.

I love working the women's fights. They bang each other out and I end up working just as many, or even more cuts with them as I do with the guys.

Bec got swollen, so I entered the cage to work on her. Bec is from Australia, and I heard her say to her coach in her accent, "I got kneed in the vagina…and it hurt!"

I didn't know how to respond to that. I wondered if I should put ice on it. Maybe not. Maybe I should ignore it. Maybe I should try to stop smiling about the comment.

I finally decided to just keep working on the swelling on her face. It was no doubt a comment that only a female fighter could make, and I thought it was amusing.

Later on down the road I asked Bec if I could put that in an article I was writing, and she had no problem with it.

Photo: Bec Hyatt

Invicta FC is now going strong, and it is thanks to the amazing work of Shannon Knapp and her team. She's such a dynamite lady. She's always showed a lot of respect for me and I really appreciate it. There was a point when she said, "Stitch, I know you've got your own line of tape, and if you ever want to put your Stitch Premium on the canvas I'd be more than glad to do that."

How awesome is that?

Everybody that fights under Invicta will tell you that she, and her team, are top of the line people that show total respect with everybody. When the UFC let me go, Shannon asked me if I'd still be willing to work with the Invicta fights.

"Is that going to create any problems for you?" I asked.

"No, no, no, no, no, I have a lot of respect for you," she said. "You're the best at what you do and you can work as many of our shows as you want."

She's a super woman. Her and Scott Coker kind of follow the same format and do a tremendous job.

I'll continue to work the Invicta fights as long as I can. The girls fight with just as much heart and determination as the guys, and they're just as tough.

Really, anybody in the sport of MMA has to be tough. It's one of the most grueling sports in the world. The work that it takes just to even consider stepping into the cage is grueling.

Boxing requires that same amount of grit, and I've been fortunate enough to work with some of the best boxers in the world.

PART 3:

BOXING

L ong before MMA, I was involved in kickboxing and then boxing. I still remember that night at the Solano County Fairgrounds so long ago. I'd been working with world champion kickboxer, Dennis Alexio. He was scheduled to fight in the main event, but before that I was cornering one of his training partners, David Rooney.

He got cut during the fight and I found myself trying to figure out how to stop the bleeding. It was the first cut I ever worked on. Afterward, when I put a butterfly bandage on the cut, David said, "Looks like you saved me some stitches… I'm going to call you Stitch."

My nickname stuck, and with it I developed a burning desire to become a cutman. Soon I found myself working with Tony Lopez, and it was with him in Monterrey, Mexico when I met the great Emanuel Steward.

My new profession eventually led me to Las Vegas where I bounced around the gyms meeting people and trying my best to learn to be a great cutman. My first payday in Vegas came with Terry Davis.

After that, I worked with guys like Ray Lovato, Mike McCallum, and Raul Marquez. These fighters, and my early days in boxing, helped me become who I am today. It was also during this time when I really began to understand that the boxing world was full of seedy, money-hungry people who preyed on the guys with the guts to climb in the ring.

Only a tiny percentage of boxers actually make big money. Most of them are used up by the worst of the promoters and spit out once it is realized that they don't have what it takes to reach star status.

The road to becoming a star is about as rough as they come. I decided that I needed to do something to educate young boxers on the ins and outs of the sport. This led to a partnership with John Barnthouse. We went to work on a documentary that would be called, *A Boxer's Nightmare*.

We interviewed so many important people in the boxing industry, including Marc Ratner, Emanuel Steward, Chuck Bodak, Fernando Vargas, and Mike Tyson. The list could go on and on. Unfortunately, the documentary could not get any traction with the promoters and the people who could get it on TV. They saw the documentary as a threat. It never saw the light of day, but I was even more determined to make a difference in the cutman profession.

The guys I work with now, the ones I'll tell stories about over the next few chapters, are some of the best in the sport. They fought their way through the nightmare and emerged as stars.

I started working with Wladimir and Vitali Klistschko in 2004. It came about after Wladimir lost to Lamon Brewster. Wladimir totally gassed in the fight and was KO'd in the fifth. Joe Souza was his cutman at the time. It was decided that him putting Vaseline on Wladimir's legs had caused him to gas.

They fired Joe. I didn't agree with it and Joe is a legendary cutman, but it opened the door for me. I actually called Joe to let him know when I got the offer to work with the Klitschkos.

I'd first met Wladimir when I played his cutman on *Ocean's*

11. He asked Emanuel Steward to contact me, and in October 2004 I worked Wladimir's corner when he fought DaVarryl Williamson at Caesar's Palace.

I've been working with the Klitschkos ever since, and it has been a truly incredible experience. They are great boxers, of course, and they are also tremendous people and businessmen. I owe a lot to Wladimir and Vitali.

Way back when I was at King's Gym in Oakland there was this young kid named Andre Ward. At the time, I sold M&M boxing equipment. I got Andre and his brother a nice pair of boxing shoes, and he always told me that when he turned pro he wanted me to be his cutman.

He was such a great kid, and he had tremendous skills. He went on to win Olympic Gold in 2004, and shortly after that he turned pro. True to his word from those days at King's Gym, Andre brought me on as his cutman. I've been with him ever since and worked all of his fights except for two.

Beibut Shumenov is a horse of a different color. I ran into him and his brother, Chingas, at a Top Rank boxing gym. We talked and hit it off. Beibut has an amazing story. He almost died as a child and grew up poor. After the Soviet Union fell, his parents rose to become one of the wealthiest families in Kazakhstan. Beibut became a lawyer and still works in the family business.

He got a title shot against Gabriel Campillo early on in his career, and brought me on to be his cutman. In the dressing room, I said, "Don't worry. I'm going to take care of you like my son."

He really took that to heart. He got poked or punched in the eye and couldn't really see. He was ready to quit. I came forward to work on him and said, "Don't worry about it. I'm going to clean you up and you'll be alright."

He ended up winning the fight. This lead to a great relationship with Beibut, and one of my favorite boxing stories ever happened when I worked with him in Kazakhstan.

With each of these guys, the Klitschkos, Andre Ward, and Beibut Shumenov, I have very different beginnings. But the one thing that is common with all of them is I really have always tried to take care of them like they were my sons, and there is no doubt that I owe a lot to them for giving me the opportunity to work in their corners.

Boxing has had its ups and downs over the years. There have been larger-than-life fighters who demanded the attention of fans from around the world, and there have been ugly controversies that have soiled the sport. But when you get in that corner and your man does his best to claim victory, all the outside distractions fall to the wayside.

As the fight unfolds, it's all that matters.

11 PLANES, TRAINS, AND AUTOMOBILES
PART ONE

T he plane drifted downward through an ever-thickening fog. Icy water coursed over the plane's windows, and then with a thump we met the runway. We'd just touched down in Almaty, Kazakhstan. It was January 2011, and it had already been a long trip. We had one more leg to go from Almaty to Shymkent, where Beibut Shumenov was scheduled to fight WBO champ, Jürgen Brähmer.

As we entered the terminal in Almaty to catch our connecting flight, I could feel the chill of the icy air cutting into my bones. I knew it would be cold, but damn, it was freaking freezing! The temperature was hanging right around zero degrees Fahrenheit. And remember, I live in Las Vegas where a sixty-degree day requires a parka.

Our group consisted of me, fellow cutman Mike Afanasiev, PR man Bob Trieger, Mexican boxer Jose Luis Cruz, and his coach. The five of us shuffled through the airport to make our connecting flight while the fog seemed to be trying to push its way in through the windows.

We got to our gate to learn that the flight had been delayed due to the fog. Almaty is in the southeastern corner of Kazakhstan.

It isn't exactly westernized, and there wasn't a whole lot of English speaking going on.

They needed us to fill out some paperwork, but of course we didn't know what the hell it said. Finally, a guy came along who could help us. He told us what they needed, and we were able to fill everything out.

We gave him twenty bucks for helping us, and he shook his head. "No, I want forty."

We all looked at each other like can you believe this guy. We told him he'd have to be happy with twenty, but he disagreed.

A moment later, a security guy with an AK-47 strapped to his chest came by. The man said something to him. He looked at the five of us and then stood next to the guy while glaring at us.

Forty bucks it was.

Keep in mind, we're here for Beibut Shumenov's fight. As I briefly mentioned before, Beibut is now a lawyer as well as a fighter. When he was a baby, and Kazakhstan was still part of the Soviet Union, his father was an accountant for the government. Beibut was staying with his aunts while his parents were away for business, and he drank spoiled milk. He got horribly sick, and was rushed to the hospital. He wasn't expected to live, but he did.

After the incident and when he got a little older, he was told that he would always be small and weak. He shouldn't do anything physical.

Then the Soviet Union fell and his parents were out of work. He was only nine years old and they were desperate to find a place to live and food to eat. His parents kept working hard despite the struggles, and slowly built up what can now be called an empire. They are some of the wealthier people in Kazakhstan with many stores and construction businesses. And with a former government background and their financial might, this created friendships with high-ranking government officials, including Prime Minister Karim Massimov and President Nursultan Nazarbayev.

But yeah, we still got hustled for forty bucks!

Anyway, one hour turned to two, and two turned to four as we sat around the airport waiting to fly to Shymkent. Finally, after about ten hours, we were in contact with Beibut's people and they came to pick us up.

They took us to a hotel in Almaty called Rixos. I've been all over the world. I've probably stayed in three thousand hotels, but none of them have been as gorgeous as the Rixos. It was like a palace.

They told us to order whatever we want and charge it to the room.

Later, Bob Trieger said, "That's the first time I ever had caviar!"

Eventually, they informed us that the fog was lifting and we were going to head back to the airport for our final leg to Shymkent. It was about four in the morning when they told us to get ready in a hurry. I felt like I was in the military again. We grabbed our stuff and headed out the doors of the beautiful Rixos and into the biting cold.

I was ready to get on that plane and get to Shymkent. I'd been traveling for over two days now.

I planned on pulling a blanket up to my chin and catching a nap on the way.

None of that shit ever happened.

12 PLANES, TRAINS, AND AUTOMOBILES PART TWO

We arrived at the airport long before the sun even considered rising from the eastern horizon. The place was nearly empty, and those who were there for their early flights moved like zombies.

Our plane was delayed, and then it was delayed some more. We sat at the damn airport for most of the morning. I found myself dreaming about that soft warm bed at the Rixos.

Finally, somebody gathered us around. "We've arranged for you to take a train to Shymkent."

"A train? How long will it take?" I asked.

He shrugged. "About fourteen hours."

Oh, damn! What was supposed to be nothing more than an hour-and-a-half flight had turned into a fourteen-hour train ride through the frozen tundra of Kazakhstan.

There wasn't anything else we could do and we had to get to Shymkent, so we trudged off behind the guy to catch our ride to the train station.

When we arrived at the station, the guy directed us to our train. At first I was sure it was a joke, but then I realized that he didn't have a sense of humor. I kid you not, it was a 1950s Soviet style train. The outside was all metal. It still had the star and the hammer and sickle emblazoned on the side. It had a coal heating system. Literally guys shoveled coal into a big furnace.

The hammer and sickle was originally designed to stand for the worker-peasant alliance. As I boarded that train I sure as hell felt like a peasant.

The rooms were about six by six with four beds. Bob Trieger said, "It's like a prison cell."

I think prison cells are a little roomier. Four of us couldn't even fit in it, so we took turns standing in the hallway with the door open.

And the toilet, it was probably the most disgusting toilet I'd ever seen. And I've seen some nasty shit. When I woke up that morning I'd peed in a lavish toilet at the hotel, now I dared not touch any surface of the shit-stained bathroom. I did glance down the hole. The ground rumbled by under my feet.

I settled in with my parka wrapped around me and my Tapout beanie pulled down low on my head. Gloves were on my hands, but the cold still seeped into my bones. It was brutal. Streams of wind cut through the corners of the windows and created a whistling sound that could be heard over the chugging of the engine.

We were in the middle of nowhere when the train slowed to a stop. I looked out the window and saw sparks everywhere. Oh crap! This old train is on fire! At least that's what I thought. It turned out to be something with the cables that created the sparks when the train slowed.

With the fears of fire still in my head, the train settled onto the tracks. I couldn't see anything but frozen ground all around us. To this day I'm not sure why we stopped, but we all got out and stretched our legs.

My bones ached and I couldn't stop shivering.

Upon boarding the train once again, we all just stood in the hallway. We'd been cramped in that room for so long it was like none of us wanted to go back in it. A few cubes away there was a group of kids with their teacher. They spoke a little bit of English and wanted to talk once they found out we spoke English.

We spent much of the rest of the trip hanging out with the kids and talking to them. They didn't seem quite as cold as I did. I guess they were used to negative four hundred degree temperatures on a metal lumbering can.

After fourteen agonizing hours, we made it to Shymkent. I was desperate for some warmth and a little bit of rest.

Then we were given some really bad news. Jürgen Brähmer had dropped out of the fight without warning. He didn't even tell promoter Dan Goossen until he was on the plane back to Germany. He'd said he got sick and had diarrhea. I'm sure he was sick, but I also think that it's possible that the absolute freezing cold weather played a part in his dropping from the fight.

This was a huge blow for Beibut. He was coming home as the champion, and he was co-promoting through his KZ Event Productions. The prime minister was even planning on attending the title fight.

It seemed all was lost, but then William Joppy saved the day by stepping in to fight Beibut.

All that waiting in the airport and traveling through the frozen tundra was not a lost cause. I'd get to work a fight after all.

13 ROYALTY

The day before the fight they got a nightclub for us. They actually ran out the people who were there. There were maybe twelve of us in all, and we had the club to ourselves. Believe it or not, there we were in Shymkent, Kazakhstan, and they had a live Cuban band playing for us. It was like night and day after that train ride. We'd gone from being the peasants to being royalty.

We ate from a big spread and drank vodka while recounting the trials and tribulations of the airport and train. I now know why they drink vodka over there. It makes you at least feel like you're warm.

I can't make this up. The fight took place in the Ice Palace. It was a boxing club turned ice skating rink and now it hosts a variety of sports. It was almost as cold in there as it had been on the train. Despite the temperature, the fight was a hot ticket. Prime Minister Karim Massimov and many other dignitaries were in attendance, and security was tight.

There was literally a security guard about every ten feet around the arena floor. Joppy had been scheduled to fight Gayrat Ahmedov, so he was in shape and ready to go.

Every time Beibut landed a crisp shot, the crowd let loose. He started timing his jab and Joppy didn't have much of an answer. In the fifth, Beibut dropped him with a big right. Then, to the delight of the Prime Minister and all the rest of the fans, he stopped him in the sixth.

I have huge respect for William Joppy for stepping up to the fight and then making Beibut work for it. Somebody else I have respect for is Jose Luis Cruz. He's the boxer that had to endure the planes and trains with us.

I know how stiff and sore my body was when we arrived in Shymkent. I'm sure his was the same, but he fought Ravshan Hudaynazarov in the co-main event. Cruz was dropped in the first thanks to a brutal liver shot, but he got back up and fought on.

Unfortunately for my travel partner, he suffered a huge cut above his right eye and the fight was stopped in the tenth.

After Beibut's victory we were treated to a party. And it wasn't just any party. It was in an immaculate room and the spread was something you'd see in a movie. Caviar and horsemeat, a delicacy there, and mountains of food covered the table. And the vodka, my God, the vodka.

There were many VIPs there. We were having a good time rubbing shoulders with them and telling stories. We were royalty once again, and I was thinking that I could definitely get used to this lifestyle.

And then as the party was winding down, they rounded us up. It was like another Army recall. They told us to get our stuff and it was time to go in an hour. It was like three in the morning. I couldn't believe we were about to leave.

I looked at all that caviar still on the table and then down at the shot of vodka in my hand. I downed it and headed for the door.

It sucked having to leave so abruptly, but I was sure that the plane ride back wouldn't be even close to as bad as the train ride there.

14 PLANES, TRAINS, AND AUTOMOBILES
PART THREE

The Siberian Express, that's what Bob called it.

Once again, we couldn't fly. They chartered a bus back to Almaty for twelve of us. This time it would take about sixteen hours.

I stood outside of the bus and pulled my Tapout beanie down low. I didn't want to get on. Maybe I should just pay for my own room until flights were available? But then again, who knew how long that would be, and I had other fights to work.

I climbed the steps of the bus and a faint nasty smell, like the remnants of barf mixed with piss, tickled my nostrils. I squinted against it and settled into a seat near the front. This bus was so damn far back. It was grimy and worn and I was sure that when it wasn't hauling us it was hauling pigs and cows.

The only saving grace was that the bus was a little warmer than the train, and by a little warmer I mean it was probably twenty degrees inside. Somebody from the back tried to take a leak, and yelled, "The damn toilet is broken."

The driver just smiled and shrugged, as if to say, of course it is.

I held out as long as I could, but nature was calling. I had a big two-liter plastic coke bottle. I worked for a few minutes to tear off the top. That became my toilet. And let me tell you, it's no fun at all to try to pee into a two-liter bottle while on a moving bus in the freezing cold.

The bus broke down twice along the way. The driver had to get out and mess with the engine until he finally got it going again. As we sat there on the broken and stinky bus, I really wondered if we'd make it to Almaty. We were once again in the middle of nowhere. It's not like we could just call for highway assistance.

Luckily, the driver had obviously dealt with mechanical problems before. Probably many times.

After the second breakdown it was like he was in a hurry to make up for lost time. He was tailgating a car and couldn't have been more than three feet away from the bumper. Mike Afanasiev and I were talking about how close he was.

Our driver muttered something under his breath that was directed at the driver in the car in front of us.

Jose Luis Cruz's boxing coach was sitting just behind us. All a sudden, he said "Come on. These are people, not chickens!"

Mike and I looked at each other and cracked up. We couldn't stop laughing. I don't know why he came up with that phrase, but I've said it many times since then and it makes me laugh every time.

We stopped to eat, and again they had horsemeat. I just couldn't do it and passed on eating it. Even though there was no bathroom on the bus, I passed on peeing as well. The "bathroom" was nothing more than a concrete slab with a hole in it. I couldn't imagine peeing in that hole in the freezing cold. I guess the two-liter bottle wasn't so bad after all.

We finally made it to the airport just before our flight. As I leaned back on the plane I couldn't help but think about all we'd been through in the last few days. What an experience. We went from being peasants to royalty to back to peasants. Kazakhstan has some beautiful cities, and no doubt they know how to host a party. They just need to figure out their transportation or build a machine that eliminates fog.

But all in all I'd say it was a successful trip. It's just one I don't really want to do again unless it's from the comfort of a plane, or maybe in the spring.

15 ANDRE WARD

Andre Ward just doesn't look like a fighter. He definitely doesn't look like a great fighter, but he is. He's such a great human being as well. A lot of media and some other boxers don't like the way Andre fights, but maybe that's because he just doesn't seem like a prototypical balls-to-the-wall fighter.

As I mentioned, I've known Andre for a long time. I first met him when he was training with his godfather, Virgil Hunter, way back in the early '90s at King's. He was always a friendly and fun kid who was ready to learn. He had a special gift for being willing to drill and drill and drill until he got every movement just right. I guess you could say he's a perfectionist, and it showed even back then. Of course some of this work ethic is directly attributed to Virgil Hunter.

When Andre was only a year or two into his boxing career, he was maybe eleven years old, he lost a couple smokers. Nobody wants to lose, but it was probably the best thing that could have happened to him.

The losses sparked a fire that couldn't be put out. He won every fight after that. As a matter of fact, after thirty pro fights he still hasn't lost since those smokers.

I watched him win the gold in Athens, and I couldn't have

been prouder. It wasn't long after that when he asked me to be his cutman. I was honored.

I gained a whole new level of respect for Andre when he fought Mikkel Kessler in the first round of the super six. Kessler was the big favorite. He'd been knocking people out like crazy.

As soon as the fight started I had my swabs ready and I was on the edge of my seat. I stayed that way until the last minute of the last round. The fight was stopped due to Kessler's cuts and went to the scorecard. I was sure that at some point Andre would get hurt. He didn't. Instead, he dominated the fight and exploited every opening in Kessler's defenses.

It was a couple fights before Andre beat Kessler when I had another leap in my respect for him. He was fighting Edison Miranda, and Miranda tried to take Andre out of his game plan. Andre got cut with a head butt in the first minute of the fight, and Miranda was really trying to roughhouse him. I watched the clock tick away as I waited to work on Andre's blood-covered face.

The round ended and I went to work. The cut was above his left eye, but it wasn't terrible. I was able to keep it under control for the rest of the fight. Andre shifted his game plan, but didn't change it. He got in the trenches with Miranda and roughhoused with him.

I was thinking to myself that he adjusted really well. He recognized the need to shift and he was able to do it.

Even though people say that he's not really a fighter, I know he has it in him. The Miranda fight was proof of that. Some people are just able to rise to meet whatever comes at them. Andre is able to do this. Sure, he's a very skilled and technical boxer, but when it comes down to it he does what it takes to win.

I worked Andre Berto's corner when he fought Victor Ortiz. In the locker room I was wrapping his hands. This was Berto's first fight after losing to Floyd Mayweather. Andre Ward was standing across the room and watching me wrap Berto's hands. Out of the blue he said, "You know, when I got cut I thought wow, I'm cut. Then it flashed through my head not to worry because I have Stitch in my corner. I just feel so confident when you work with me."

It made me feel so damn good, because one of the biggest parts of my job is to make every fighter I work with feel confident. I want them to be one hundred percent sure that I'll take care of them.

Andre finished up by saying, "Man, I love you, Stitch."

"That's pretty awesome," I replied. "You know I love you, too."

He said all of this loud enough so everyone could hear, and I'm sure it helped put Andre Berto's mind at ease. That's the kind of kid Andre Ward is. He's a pleasure to work with and I'm proud to be a part of his career.

It wasn't long after this moment when I walked into the dressing room in preparation for Andre's fight with Alexander Brand. I sat side by side with Andre and told him how important those words were to me.

His next fight, at the time of this writing, will be against Sergey Kovalev. He's an as-tough-as-they-come Russian and pound for pound one of the best. I wanted to assure Andre that I will be there every minute of every round. My goal is to keep him looking as handsome during the fight as he is coming into it.

16 THE KLITSCHKOS

Wladimir and Vitali Klitschko are two of the most incredible people I've ever met. And I'm not even talking about their boxing abilities. Of course they are great boxers. Each of their careers stacks up against the best heavyweights to ever fight.

What I'm talking about is the Klitschkos outside of the ring. I started working with them back in 2004 during a time of real political strife in their home country of Ukraine. I'm not going to spend a lot of time on it because I covered it in my first book, but they were integral in the Orange Revolution, a series of political events and protests against widespread voter fraud and corruption surrounding an election.

Since I worked Vitali's fight during this time, I put on my orange outfit like everyone else. I remember sitting there ringside at the Mandalay Bay watching him dismantle Danny Williams. I was thinking how different these two were. They are so much more than boxers. They care deeply about their country, and they not only want what is best for it, but are willing to go out and make a difference. Vitali has said that change can only be made from the inside. He ran for mayor of Kiev twice, losing both times, but came back and won the election in 2014. He's been elected to the Ukrainian Parliament and created a political party in an effort to change the future of his country.

Wladimir, who is about four years younger than his brother, is not quite as into politics, but he is active and of course supports Vitali.

Here's a story that most people probably don't know about Wladimir. In March 2012, I was in Germany working with him when he knocked out Jean-Marc Mormeck. It was another spectacular performance by Wladimir, but what happened not long after that fight is truly one for the books.

Wladimir decided to auction off the gold medal he won in Atlanta in the 1996 Olympics. This is something he treasured and as he's said to me before, "It [the medal] was the foundation for my professional success."

And yet he was willing to auction it off to help thousands of underprivileged kids in Ukraine. The winning bid was right around one million dollars!

Here's where the story gets even better. The winning bidder then returned the medal explaining that he wanted it to stay with the Klitschkos.

Since I've known Wladimir and Vitali I've always marveled at their willingness to help others. In this instance the favor was returned and it was a perfect case of instant karma.

They've constantly supported or created charities that have helped kids around the world, and they don't do it just to make themselves look good. They do it to truly help others.

Wladimir's nickname is Dr. Steelhammer. Vitali's nickname is Dr. Ironfist. And that's because they have earned PhD's in sports science. They both speak Ukrainian, Russian, German, and English, and they are adept businessmen. They have an athlete management company, own hotels, have worked in the film industry, the list goes on and on.

They truly are the most professional people I've ever had the pleasure of knowing.

They love playing chess, and are very good, and Wladimir often talks about his passion for golf. The one thing that kind of seems out of place is their boxing career, and yet that is what gave them the ability to create all these other amazing aspects to their lives.

Wladimir definitely has the more outgoing personality. I'll never forget the time not long after they brought me on board. We were at a Japanese restaurant in Hamburg, Germany when he asked me what I thought of them letting their former cutman, Joe Souza, go. I told him that I thought it was a mistake and they fired the wrong person for the wrong reason.

Wladimir looked at me for a moment and then smiled. "You got big balls, Stitch," he said.

"I'm always going to be honest," I replied.

I think that Wladimir really appreciated that. Maybe it was risky for me to say it, but I wanted to be up front with him. If he was a lesser man he might have become angry and told me to get my ass back on a plane to Vegas, but he didn't.

The Klitschkos have the utmost respect for honesty, and they are about as upstanding and honest as somebody could be.

Vitali has a more closed personality. He is stoic and carries himself much more in the eastern European way, serious and focused.

In October 2013, Wladimir had a huge fight against Alexander Povetkin in Moscow. It was intense, and he claimed the unanimous decision. Afterward, we were saying our goodbyes and Vitali said, "Stitch, I'm not gay, but I love you."

It was pretty funny coming from Vitali, and I took it with a lot of heart because of who he is and how big he is. The other thing he has said to me that I take as a very high compliment is that if I was with him when he fought Lennox Lewis he would have won.

In Moscow when Wladimir fought Povetkin, I was sitting in

the lobby of the hotel with Vitali. He talked about his father, who was a Soviet Air Force major general. In 1986, he was one of the first responders of the Chernobyl Nuclear Disaster and commanded much of the cleanup. At the time, Vitali was fourteen years old, and Wladimir was ten. They lived on a military base about an hour away from the disaster. Their dad spent months there.

He passed away due to cancer in 2011. He was only sixty-four years old. The doctors told Vitali that it was due to exposure to nuclear fallout. I sat there in the immaculate hotel and listened as Vitali recounted the events and talked about how he cried and cried upon finding out.

It is hard for me to imagine him crying, but they had so much respect for their father and loved him dearly.

This led to talk of politics, and Vitali told me about how after his father passed his mother went to the government for the money that was due thanks to his father's service. They told her that they didn't have any money available. She tried to protest, but got nowhere. She left, and was obviously sad. A man approached her and said, "Ms. Klitschko, I can get you the money, but it will cost you fifty percent."

Vitali shook his head back and forth in disgust when he told me that last part, and then said, "That's the kind of corruption that we have in our country, and I want to eliminate it."

Now Vitali is the mayor of Kiev, and I would expect that one day he will be the president of the country. I'm sure his political career will be every bit as successful as his boxing career, and he will make great strides toward eliminating corruption and making his country better.

It has been such an honor working with both of them, even if I didn't get to stay in the Hyatt in Moscow!

17 THE HYATT

Prior to the aforementioned fight between Wladimir and Alexander Povetkin, I got the message that we'd be staying in the Ararat Park Hyatt in Moscow. I did a quick search to check it out. The hotel was absolutely gorgeous, and it was located next to the Kremlin, the Red Square, and Saint Basil's Cathedral.

I was pretty excited to stay in such a nice place close to so many landmarks. The driver took me to the Hyatt and I took in the sights as he drove. He pulled into the hotel and I hopped out and made my way through the beautiful lobby to the check-in desk.

"Jacob Duran, checking in. It's under the Klitschkos," I said.

"I'm sorry, Mr. Duran," the lady said, "but the Klitschkos moved their camp to a different hotel."

I was disappointed to not be staying at the Hyatt, but I was there to work so I shrugged it off. The driver pulled away from the hotel and we drove and drove.

The buildings thinned out, and soon we were actually outside of the city. He kept going. "This is it. He's going to murder me out here in the fields," I thought to myself.

Finally, we pulled into a hotel that was really in the middle of nowhere. I felt like I was in the shining because there were maybe three or four other people staying in the entire hotel, and then there was our group. It was pretty eerie in that empty hotel, and there was nothing for me to do.

The Klitschkos brought everything: mattresses, bedding, towels, and food. Literally anything you can think of, they brought it. They did this for security reasons.

This was a big fight with the Russian, Povetkin against the Ukrainian, Klitschko. There was concern that somebody would try to do something to sway the fight in Povetkin's favor.

I remember at the briefings regarding the walk to the ring they were going to have smoke. This is pretty standard with big boxing entrances, but Klitschko's management said, "No smoke."

They were concerned that something could be put in it that would affect Wladimir. That's how high their level of concern was. They planned on coming through the back to get to the ramp that would lift him for the entrance. I mean it was that crazy. Every possible detail was covered to ensure that Wladimir would make it the ring unscathed.

Finally, it was time for the fight, and who do I run into? Fedor Emelianenko.

Fedor and I go way back to the PRIDE days. The first time I wrapped his hands he looked at the wraps and raised his hands, clenching and unclenching them, and then he looked at me and said one word, "Super."

I felt like I was on cloud nine after receiving that one-word compliment from none other than "The Last Emperor."

Later, I drank Vodka with him after one of his fights and we have been friends ever since.

What a great surprise it was to run into him. I guess it made sense that he would be at this huge fight in Moscow, but it still surprised me. It's funny because in my MMA outfits I'm always wearing black, and of course Fedor is always wearing red. Well, it turned out on this night that I was the one in red since I was working with Wladimir, and Fedor was dressed in black pants and a black jacket. We made a couple jokes about it and talked for a bit. He introduced me to a few people and it was a nice moment away from the tension of the upcoming fight.

When Wladimir and Povetkin did get into the ring, Wladimir beat him pretty handily in an ugly fight.

Afterward, we made our way back to our hotel in the middle of nowhere, and I got ready for the flight home. It was a shame because I was very much looking forward to seeing Moscow. Hopefully one day I'll be able to go back.

I don't know if it will happen since Vitali has retired and Wladimir is reaching the end of his career. If it doesn't, I'll still have hundreds of great memories thanks to the Klitschkos.

PART 4:

BEHIND THE SCENES

When it comes to combat sports, all eyes are plastered on the cage or ring. Everybody can understand a fight. Two guys, or girls throw down and we have a clear-cut winner or loser unless it's a controversial decision. It's usually obvious that one person beat the other, and often they have displayed so much skill and heart that the fans have a real appreciation for their efforts.

The fight is the culmination of so much training: blood, sweat, tears, hours in the gym, sleepless nights as the fight runs through the head, hope, fear. The list of preparation and pain is long, and it's all for that moment when two people touch gloves and then fight.

It's really a beautiful thing when you think about it. There's a pureness to it, and it forces men and women to reach down deep to really find out what they are made of.

What many fight fans might not fully understand is just how much goes into the show, how much has to be done behind the scenes and all the people that are involved. Us cutmen are seen in the ring or cage fixing cuts, but there is much more to our job that isn't seen. And it's not just cutmen who put in a lot of work behind the scenes.

Throughout my career I've been blessed to work with so many tremendous professionals who have become great friends. I'd like to talk about some of them because they are instrumental in combat sports.

18 LEON TABBS

I met Leon at UFC 33, the first show I worked for the promotion. He'd been working for the UFC since the very beginning. We like to refer to him as the Godfather of MMA cutmen. He's an old school cutman who didn't like to give away his secrets. It made sense, because he worked in the boxing industry for a long time. The history and knowledge he has runs deep.

He's from Philadelphia and boxed as a kid. He became a Navy medic during the Korean War, and when he returned he was a cop in Philly. All the while, he kept training boxers. He became well known in Philly, and then Sylvester Stallone came along with *Rocky*. Leon got a part in the movie.

He's worked with so many amazing boxers, including Bernard Hopkins, and like I said, he was with the UFC since the beginning.

At first, I wasn't sure how we'd be together. I'm more of a new-school cutman and have no problem telling people how I do what I do. But Leon and I soon became great friends and were a formidable team when it came to wrapping hands and fixing cuts.

I once said to Leon, "How is it that an East Coast brother from Philadelphia is best friends with a Mexican farm worker from the West Coast?

He laughed and said, "No shit."

His way of approving.

Anybody in the industry knows Leon's famous words. He's the man who would give you a sideways glance and his voice would raise just a bit before he'd say, "No shit!"

I mentioned it in the first book, but I'll never forget when Evan Tanner fought David Loiseau in 2005. Evan was busted up, five cuts on his face. I was trying to work on all these cuts when like an Angel from Heaven, Leon appeared and helped me take care of Evan.

Leon and I have traveled the world together as we have worked fights. We were in Sydney, Australia eating Chinese food. You know those real dry hot peppers they put in the food for flavoring? Well, I looked over at Leon and he was sweating bullets.

"Leon, what's wrong?" I asked.

"Man, these peppers are hot."

"Shit, you're not supposed to eat them," I said. "Those are just to give it flavor."

He didn't say it, because his mouth was on fire, but I'm sure he was thinking, no shit.

I never laughed so hard in my life. The look on Leon's face was priceless.

One time we were working in Chicago and Leon, Don House, and I were walking down Madison Avenue. This lady was on her phone and she hurried up to us. "Excuse me, Geraldo, can you talk to my mother?" she said to me.

"I'm sorry, but I'm not Geraldo," I replied.

She looked confused for a moment and then apologized as Leon and Don laughed about it.

I put that out on a Tweet, and somebody replied. "With you three walking on the street it could have been Geraldo Rivera (me), Sugar Ray Leonard (House), and Morgan Freeman (Leon)."

I thought that was funny as hell, and we do each have a resemblance to the abovementioned.

One of the ways I wanted to honor Leon for his amazing career as a cutman was to have the UFC recognize him at UFC 100. I always tried to promote Leon, even if he didn't really want it. I mentioned to some of the UFC people about honoring him because he was the last one of the originals from the first UFC, and he was still there at 100. I thought it would be great if they could recognize him, or even put him into the Hall of Fame.

None of that ever happened. They just weren't interested. Luckily, Fighters Only started their World MMA Awards not long before this. I've had a long relationship with the magazine, having written for them for many years. I talked to owner, Rob Hewitt, about the possibility of doing something for Leon.

He liked the idea, and decided that he'd give him a lifetime achievement award. Our concern was that Leon wouldn't come to Las Vegas to receive the award because he shied away from the spotlight.

"How are we going to get him to come to Vegas?" Rob asked.

"I'm going to have to lie to him. If I tell him he's getting an award there's no way he'll come."

I gave Leon a call and told him that Fighters Only wanted to acknowledge us, along with Don House, because we'd been cutmen with the UFC for the longest period of time. Fighters Only was paying for his flight and I'd really like him to come.

He said he would.

During the awards, we all sat at the same table. It's always quite the affair. Everyone is dressed sharp and they do a tremendous job putting on the show. Rob was at the podium and he started introducing the lifetime achievement award.

Leon sat there not thinking much about it because he thought they were giving the award to me.

Then Rob said, "The lifetime achievement award goes to

Leon Tabbs."

Leon looked at Don and me, and then what does he say over the thunderous applause? "No shit!"

He got up there and gave a little speech, and it was a great tribute to the man that I've always respected. He really is the Godfather of cutmen in mixed martial arts.

It was a pleasure to work with him for so many years.

19 BURT WATSON

Joe Rogan gave Burt Watson the title of Babysitter to the Stars. It's a fitting name.

For the longest time, Burt Watson and the Buffalo Soldiers, the guys that worked with him, were the unsung heroes. It didn't matter where the fights were. They could literally be anywhere in the world, and the first to arrive to start setting everything up were Burt and his crew.

Before any fighters arrived, Burt was there working his fingers to the bone. He made sure the training facilities were set up, the rooms were arranged, the pick-up times at the airport were correct. You name it, Burt and his guys did it to ensure everything ran smoothly.

Once the fighters arrived, Burt got them on the scales and worked hard to ensure they were on track for making weight. He was always encouraging and always energetic. He worked his ass off, and he did it on a weekly basis from one fight to the next to the next.

It wasn't until they brought Burt onto the stage at the weigh-ins when people really got a glimpse of just how much he did. Still, I think very few really understood the extent of his importance.

Burt always made the fighters feel good and energized. His

big line was, and still is, "Let's roll, Baby!"

I bet I heard him say this a thousand times, and it never got old.

Another thing that he routinely said to the fighters was, "Don't leave it in the hands of the judges because they'll make you cry."

Burt, his Buffalo Soldiers, and the cutmen were the nuts and bolts of a fight night. No doubt about it. He was our leader, and we'd follow him anywhere.

It was UFC 184 when everything went to hell. It all started with Mark Munoz missing weight and staying behind to re-weigh. Somehow he didn't have a ride back to the hotel and was left for about an hour. Burt and Mark saw each other at the hotel afterward, and everything was fine.

It was a little later when Burt got a call from a UFC official. I know who, but he never would divulge the official's name, and neither will I. He did say that it wasn't the Fertittas, or Dana White or Donna Marcolini, and that they were always good to him. I will say that we often had issues with this official's harshness. Burt was disrespected, and he is a man of his principles. He quit the next day.

When he said that he was done, a lot of people thought that he'd come back. I was sure he wouldn't. When Burt decided on something, it was a done deal.

Many people blamed Mark Munoz for him leaving, but Burt is quick to say that it was absolutely nothing that Mark did that led to his decision to leave. I've known Mark for a long time. He is a stand-up guy, and I'm sure that he did not push the issue. Maybe he was upset for being stuck at the venue, but he would never whine about it.

The outpouring of support for Burt was pretty spectacular. I'm glad that the fans had begun to really understand just how important he was when it came to making sure each show ran smoothly.

It was really sad to see him go. He was an inspiration to everyone, and he also kept everyone in line. I'll never forget the time we were heading to a weigh-in. All the fighters except for one were on the bus and waiting. Burt asked where the last guy was, and somebody said he was still in the lobby taking pictures and signing autographs.

In and of itself this isn't a big deal. One of the great things about MMA is how connected the fighters are with the fans. But in this instance it was time to get to the weigh-in, and this guy was making everybody wait.

He'd been on a TUF show and was still one of the rookies in the UFC. Burt got off the bus and headed into the lobby. He told the fighter that he might be good, but he wasn't bigger than the sport. Get on the bus.

Burt, who is a former Marine, has a profound respect for order and efficiency. He wanted everyone to do well while understanding that they were a part of something bigger. Burt is a man of integrity, and when he knew he was right he stuck by it completely.

There was one time when Burt was left shaking his head. On our return trip to the hotel after the weigh-ins in Abu Dhabi, Burt was in the lead vehicle escorting two buses filled with fighters, trainers, and the cutmen.

The two buses stopped on the side of the road. Burt's driver was unsure what happened, so he put his vehicle in reverse and rushed back to the buses.

Renzo Gracie was one of the passengers. Two souped-up sports cars flagged the buses to stop. The drivers where part of the Royal family and students of Renzo. They pulled Renzo off the bus, put him in one of the two cars and sped off to the hotel. It was special treatment for a special person.

When Burt arrived at the buses and found out what had

happened, the look on his face was priceless! What could he do? He was out ranked.

I knew him outside of the UFC because he was a coordinator for the Klitschkos. He also managed Joe Frazier and worked for Don King. He has always been a consummate professional. He was also a huge advocate for us cutmen. He understood just how important our jobs were and he knew that we were a part of his team. I've always appreciated that about him.

There is no doubt that there will never be another Burt Watson. He's still working shows and doing his thing. I hope that we will work together again in the future.

20 HUITZI MATA

I remember Arturo Mata as a young boxing trainer like myself during the late '80s in the Bay Area. We saw each other from time to time as we hustled around the boxing circuit working to make a name for ourselves. During that time we became friends.

Fast-forward to April 19, 2008, UFC 183, Serra vs. St. Pierre 2. Cain Velasquez was making his UFC debut against Brad Morris. I saw Javier Mendes and he introduced me to Cain. Arturo who was the striking coach for Cain, Mike Swick and Kyle Kingsbury were all sitting to Javier's right. I gave Arturo a handshake and hug. He told me his new name was Huitzilin Mata, and that he had been studying his Aztec culture.

In the past few years I saw Huitzi, as he liked to be called, more often since the UFC bought Strikeforce, where he'd been working as a cutman along with Ted Lucio.

We often talked about his spiritual experiences and how they had changed his life. Many times Huitzi had invited me to participate in a weekend of spiritual awakenings by attending a sweat lodge and taking Ayahuasca.

For those who don't know, Ayahuasca is an entheogenic brew, meaning "the divine within." The drink is typically made of roots and leaves from Brazil and Peru. It's used in spiritual ceremonies mainly for the purpose of achieving spiritual revelations. There are many different mixtures, and they all have psychedelic effects.

Taking Ayahuasca can lead to a really positive life-changing experience, or it can really mess you up with some psychological and emotional stress.

One of the side effects of Ayahuasca is vomiting, or purging. Shamans say this is necessary because it releases the negative energy that has built up throughout your life.

I decided that it was important for me to see the world and myself in different situations, so I took the challenge. Huitzi instructed me to eat only fruits, nuts, and greens, and drink only water during the week leading up to my journey at Indian Canyon, where the ceremonies would take place. He was my advisor and friend, so I did as he asked. He also instructed me to buy a tent, sleeping bag, and cushions.

Once we arrived at Indian Canyon, a sacred place for the Ohlone tribe, we started setting up our campsite. Being the rookie that I was, I needed help on setting up my tent.

Huitzi and others prepared the sweat lodge by placing blankets over its skeleton until the top was completely covered.

Then they went by the river and collected grass that they laid inside of the lodge. Next, they gathered wood to heat the lava rocks that would create the heat and humidity.

Night came, and so did others who would participate for these two days.

I wasn't sure what to expect, and was nervous as the ceremony grew near. The transformation of Huitzi from friend and cutman to shaman was overwhelming. As I watched his transformation, I felt like I was going to have an experience of a lifetime.

The sweat lodge was pitch black and burning hot. Sweat beaded up on my arms and ran down my neck and back. The process was designed to cleanse my body of toxins as I got to understand my inner-strength.

Barefoot, dirty, and sweaty, we sat around and shared our experiences as we anticipated the following day when we would take Ayahuasca.

The night wound down, so I said goodnight and headed for my tent. I tossed and turned for about twenty minutes as I struggled to get comfortable on the hard surface of the ground. Finally, I said screw this and left my tent to sleep in comfort of my car.

My dirty sandals and shoes were outside my car door. I woke up around three in the morning to take a leak and couldn't find one of my sandals and one of my shoes. It seems the raccoons had taken one shoe and one sandal. Luckily, I found my shoe the next morning.

With only a peach and water in my system, I joined the others to take my first drink of Ayahuasca. Not knowing what to expect, but willing to see where my mind would take me, I laid down and let the drink guide me. I saw and heard so many emotions during my journey. They rolled over me and rattled through my soul. I felt I was on a good journey.

Many were already purging, and I felt good because I kept my peach and water in my stomach, that is until I took my second shot of Ayahuasca. I sure don't know what happened next, because I had that salty taste in my mouth. I grabbed my bucket and purged a lot more than I expected. Then I went into phase two.

After six hours I had continually seen an eagle and a bear. When the effects of the Ayahuasca had worn off, I asked Huitzi to interpret my journey.

He said, "Carnal, you had a good journey. The eagle is your vision and the bear is your strength."

There was also a tiny blue light, a color blue like I have never seen before, in the far distance.

I asked Huitzi about it.

"Brother, that is the light at the end of the tunnel. You had a good trip."

Photo: Huitzi Mata

I never fully understood what Huitzi meant until I arrived in Afghanistan to visit the troops. There I really began to understand because it felt like we were on the edge of death, almost taunting it, during parts of our trip.

It was only a few years after this incredible Ayahuasca experience, in June 2016 just days before the passing of Muhammad Ali and "Kimbo Slice," when Huitzi Mata died in his sleep. I knew him in a variety of walks of life, from boxing, to being a cutman, to being a shaman. He taught me a great deal and I'll forever be grateful for his guidance and wisdom.

I found an article on MMAJunkie written by Christian Stein

that remembered Huitzi's life. Huitzi had said in an interview before his passing, "…If there's any hero that I'm going to look up to, it would be my other me. The one that gave me the advice. You know we have one friend and one enemy. And the friend, he's telling me, 'Hey, you can do it, be comfort. Nothing could happen. If you're doing this job that's because you are good at it.'

"And the other friend, 'Oh no, you might not be able to do it.' I don't listen. I just flick him [away]. So I think I look to my inner self."

Huitzi did this throughout his life on his constant quest for knowledge and enlightenment, and he gave me the gift of looking to my inner self.

He left behind his two teenage sons. They can be very proud of their father. He was a tremendous cutman and an even better person.

21 EMANUEL STEWARD

I t's tough to put it into words, but I was the most honored to be working the corner with Emanuel Steward because of all that he did and what he was known for.

He was a great amateur boxer who found his place in the world through training his brother at the famous Kronk Gym. He trained multiple champs and became well known when he worked with Thomas Hearns. For the better part of four decades he was one of the most important people in boxing.

I really knew that I was working at the highest level when Wladimir Klitschko fought Samuel Peter. It was a tough fight for Wladimir. He got dropped repeatedly thanks to some pretty suspect rabbit punches. Even as his fighter was struggling, Emanuel kept his composure. And he made sure that Wladimir kept his composure as well.

It was Emanuel, Vitali, and me working the corner, and to this day it is still the most professional corner I've ever worked because of the job Emanuel did keeping him composed and giving him strategies to hang on and eventually win.

When a fighter is in the ring, each round is three minutes of trauma. That one minute of rest is so important. It involves controlling breathing, cooling down, gaining valuable insight, and words of encouragement.

Emanuel did all of those things with such precision and calmness. Anybody who gets dropped five or six times, whatever the amount was, in a fight, shouldn't win. He did, because Emanuel kept him in the game and Wladimir showed his amazing heart and will to persevere.

It really was a great moment.

To sit there and chat with Emanuel was always a delight. Even though he was great at what he did, he was just a normal person. When Nick Ward and I had our radio show I'd call Emanuel for interviews on a fairly regular basis. No matter how busy he was, he never hesitated to come on the show.

The only time I ever saw Emanuel lose his composer was when Wladimir fought David Haye. There was some controversial stuff going on, and Emanuel lost it. After one of the rounds he jumped into the middle of the ring and yelled at the referee. I was working on Wladimir and we looked at each other like, what on earth is he doing?

My job as a cutman isn't to give instructions, but if I do say something the guys know it's important and for their best interest. "Wladimir, look man, you're doing fine."

It was a pretty simple statement meant to ensure that he would not get rattled. After the fight Wladimir mentioned it. "I remember Emanuel jumping into the middle of the ring and going after the referee, and you said, 'Don't worry, you're doing fine.' That was just what I needed to hear."

That was a small example of how we all worked together as a team, and I said it before, but it really was an honor to work with Emanuel, and this was the only time I ever saw him lose his composure.

On July 7, 2012, Wladimir fought in Bern, Switzerland and scored a TKO over Tony Thompson. Before the fight I had lunch with Emanuel. It was special because it was both his birthday and my wife, Charlotte's, birthday.

We were talking and having a great time, and I had no idea he was sick. He was smiling and as happy as usual. The next day we were hanging in the airport talking about boxing and life in general like we always did.

It was time to go so we said our goodbyes and went our separate ways. I didn't realize it would be the last time I'd see him. Not long afterward I learned he was sick, and then on October 25 he passed away.

I remember the special moments with Emanuel and marvel at how much he did for the sport of boxing. After his death, Wladimir said, "It's not often that a person in any line of work gets a chance to work with a legend. Well I was privileged enough to work with one for almost a decade. I will miss our time together. The long talks about boxing, the world, and life itself. Most of all, I will miss our friendship."

I couldn't agree more, Wladimir.

22 MARC RATNER

When I first moved to Vegas to follow my dream to become a cutman, I was still working for RJ Reynolds Tobacco Company. I was at one of my accounts, White Cross Drugs. They had a little mom-and-pop restaurant with really good food.

I was walking out of there one day when I saw Marc Ratner in the parking lot. I introduced myself to him and told him I was in Las Vegas to be a cutman. He welcomed me and wished me luck. I'm sure at the time he was thinking that it would be a long shot for me, but he never said that.

He started seeing me around more and more as I worked my way into the boxing world. He was the head of the Nevada State Athletic Commission at the time. I introduced the power flex tape to him and he approved it. We worked closely on hand wrapping often and discussed what should and should not be allowed.

When I did *A Boxer's Nightmare* with John Barnthouse, Marc gave me some of his time. I remember he talked about how the promoters and television, like HBO and Showtime, should be investing in the fighters. He believed that would make the sport better. It was very admirable of him.

Marc is such a cool and calm customer. When Mike Tyson bit

part of Evander Holyfield's ear off, it was Marc who referee Mills Lane turned to for help. Marc stepped up on the apron and told him that he had to disqualify Mike.

Lorenzo Fertitta was on the NSAC before he bought the UFC. He knew the caliber of person Marc was, and I say that them bringing Marc Ratner on as a UFC executive is the smartest move they ever made.

When Marc joined the promotion, it added an air of legitimacy. And then he went from one state to the next ensuring that MMA would be legalized. He even eventually got New York to give in.

In over twenty years I've never heard anybody say a bad word about him, and you won't hear me say anything bad about him either, because it would be untruthful.

23 THE CUTMEN

I would be remiss if I didn't talk about many of the tremendous men and women who I have worked with through the years. I talked about it in my first book, but some three decades ago when I had a burning desire to be a cutman I was stonewalled at every turn.

I asked a few cutmen to give me some pointers. Each one looked at me like I'd just peed on his carpet. Back then, it was a very secretive trade. Giving away how you wrapped hands or worked on cuts was sacrilegious.

It was like I was stuck on an island in the middle of the ocean all alone when it came to learning the trade. I remember going to the library to find books about the bones and muscles in the face and which nerves were where.

During that time I vowed that if I ever really made it in the profession I would never withhold information. I've never been scared of others taking my job because of something I have taught them. My job is to take care of the fighters. If I can do that by helping other cutmen grow, I'm all for it.

And I've learned plenty from other guys in the trade. Often people say that I'm the best in the business. I appreciate that compliment, but believe me, there are many other wonderful cutmen out there working hard at perfecting their skills.

I've had the absolute pleasure of working with many of them. I've seen guys wrap hands beautifully or fix tough cuts that have definitely saved a fight, or even a career, for the man in the ring or cage. I've also seen cutmen help calm a fighter before they step into the arena of combat.

It's a pleasure to see an organization like the International Cutman's Association where men and women from all over the world come together with the purpose of helping everyone get better.

The visionaries of the ICA are President, Federico Catizone, from Rome Italy, and Vice-President, Michael Schmidt, from Germany. Together they had a dream to bring all cutmen together and share knowledge and support each other.

I was invited to Cologne, Germany for the First Hand Wrapping Championship held during the FIBO Convention, April 3-6, 2014.

Michael Schmidt was the German host, and what a magnificent job he did. I have always said that Germany and Japan are the most organized countries in the world. Michael proved me right.

Phantom MMA was the official sponsor. They supplied the shirts for all contestants with their names on them.

Cutmen, Roland Aicher traveled from Austria, Stefan Lems from Holland, Tommy McCormick from Ireland, UFC veteran, Adam Gigli from the UK, and many more from throughout Europe.

The suave looking Italian, Federico Catizone, welcomed all the cutmen with dinner and a visual presentation on cuts and injuries.

The finale was a hand wrapping contest that attracted many of the FIBO visitors. I was a judge and glad to see so many talented cutmen competing for the title as the best of the best.

Adam Gigli took the championship honors.

During the closing ceremonies, Federico Catizone and Michael Schmidt knighted me as Honorary President of the ICA. It's a badge I wear with pride knowing that all the hard work I have put into being a cutman has made a positive impact with other cutmen around the world.

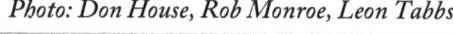

We all know that it is the fighters who make the sport. If it wasn't for them none of us would be able to do what we do. I feel like I've limited this section to just a few of the giants in the combat sports world, but there are so many other amazing people who work behind the scenes. I've been fortunate to work with some of the best cutmen in the business. Guys like Leon Tabbs, Don House, Rob Monroe, Mike Afanasiev, Michael Dreisbach, and many others.

Photo: Don House, Rob Monroe, Leon Tabbs

I've seen top-notch officiating up close and personal. I've seen coaches keep fighters in the fight. I've seen teammates pour their sweat and blood on the mat so their man or woman can have their shot at glory in the cage.

It takes a great deal of behind the scenes work so the fans can see two gladiators square off in the ring or cage. That final moment of confrontation stands on the shoulders of so many men and women who never expect any notoriety. In fact, they don't even crave it, because when two fighters put on an amazing display of heart and skill for the fans, us behind-the-scenes guys know that we played a role in making it happen.

PART 5:

SHOW BUSINESS

24 HERE COMES THE BOOM

Most people probably learned who Kevin James was from his role on *King of Queens*. That TV show aired for nine seasons, from 1998 to 2007. Kevin was hilarious as Doug Heffernan, and he often drove his way-too-hot wife, Carrie, played by Leah Remini, crazy with his antics.

Charlotte and I used to watch the show regularly. We both loved it.

Kevin was a wrestler in high school and he's a long-time MMA fan. That's why it didn't really surprise me much when I heard he was making a movie about MMA. At one of the Vegas UFCs in probably early 2011, I walked around to Don House's side of the cage. People were stopping me and asking for pictures, so of course I accommodated. Then this one guy wanted a picture of me just standing there by myself. I told him that was fine, but why not take a picture together.

He snapped the picture with us together and introduced himself as Frank Coraci, the director of Kevin's new movie, *Here Comes the Boom*. He asked if I would consider being in the movie.

"Of course," I replied, and gave him my card.

It wasn't long after that when I got a call with the offer. They were flying me first class to Boston. I'd have my own trailer at the movie set. They'd need me for this length of time. Stuff like that. It all sounded terrific to me, so I told them I was in.

I was super excited when I arrived in Boston. The filming was actually in Lowell, Massachusetts. A car took me there and lo and behold who do I see? Bruce Buffer, Herb Dean, Bas Rutten, Mark DellaGrotte, Krzysztof Soszynski, Joe Rogan, all the MMA guys.

Then I got to meet Kevin James, Henry Winkler, and finally Salma Hayek. Meeting Salma was a great moment for me. We chatted in Spanish, and it just so happened that her parents were there. She introduced me to them. She was so nice and even more beautiful in person. It was an incredible experience just getting to meet all of them, and working with them was even better.

Like I said, the filming was in Lowell, about forty minutes from where we were staying in Boston. Bas Rutten had one of the lead roles in the movie so he was scheduled to be there for three months. He had his Porsche shipped there so he could drive around. Bas and I have been friends for a long time, and he told me he'd be happy to give me a ride to the set.

We were working about fourteen hour days. I was exhausted and it was just before six in the morning. It was one of those days when the gray clouds hung just above the trees, threatening to bust open with rain at any minute. I walked out of the hotel to find Bas waiting on me.

He was just about as wired up as you could get, seriously Bas Rutten style even though it was so early. I piled into his car as the rain started to fall. He was downing an energy drink. His music was on full blast, and I made sure that my seatbelt was on real tight.

He took off like he'd just robbed a bank, and I reassured myself by realizing that as crazy as Bas is, and he has been all his life, he's still alive. I have to have confidence in his skills that we'll be getting to Lowell in one piece.

Almost every time I wanted to speak to him, I had to turn the volume down. He had so much freaking energy, and he's as awesome as they come. It was hilarious, and those rides became part of my morning routine. I didn't even need any coffee to wake up once we arrived at the set.

Just to be a part of that movie was tremendous. There was a scene when Henry Winkler is talking to Kevin James during a fight. I sat back and watched, realizing that this was my first time to really see A-level acting skills up close and personal. It was a motivational speech and it almost brought me to tears. It was a classy moment.

I was also so impressed with Kevin James. He's really athletic and has a lot of MMA and boxing skills. I didn't expect it, and I think he surprised others as well, but no doubt Kevin is an athlete. He and Krzysztof worked so well together, and Krzysztof did a great job. Really, all of the MMA guys did a great job under the direction of Frank Coraci.

Let me go back and explain a bit. When I got the script I was in a few scenes, but I didn't have any lines. I knew that if I could figure out how to get a line, I'd get residuals. I was thinking, crap, I've got to say something. For two weeks I considered what I should try to say.

I came up with an idea, but just before I was about to do my scenes with Kevin, he pulled me aside and said, "Stitch, we've got to have you say something."

That's the kind of person he is. He didn't have to give me that opportunity.

Like I said, I had an idea what I wanted to say. "How about welcome to the UFC?" I asked.

"That's great," he said.

I had my line!

In the scene, Kevin got cut, and Mark DellaGrotte called me in. Kevin looked up at me and said, "Stitch, I can't believe you're working on me, man. It's so awesome. I'm having a crazy month of meeting people."

This was my line, but I had a little trick up my sleeve. He didn't know it was coming, but as soon as I said, "Welcome to the UFC," I reached up and slapped him and walked away.

Man, everybody started laughing. Kevin thought it was great. The reason I didn't want to tell him is because I didn't want him to flinch.

"That was awesome, Stitch," Kevin said. "We can use that in the trailer!"

That was my signature moment with Kevin James, to slap him in the face. It was pretty cool. The whole experience was cool. It was a great time working with all of them, and it was such a fun movie.

Bas Rutten did a tremendous job. He was hilarious as always. There's a scene when Bas is in the studio working with all these girls. He's going through these ridiculous self-defense techniques, and he'd told me before that those techniques were actually based on a guy that came up to him in a bar way before the movie.

He told Bas that he was a badass and if he was in a street fight he'd do this and that to the guy. Punch, punch, knee, knee, elbow, elbow, that type of thing. Bas was looking at him like, what the hell, but he thought it was so funny that he decided to base the moves that he taught the girls on it.

After knowing that story, I couldn't stop laughing as I watched that scene in the movie. It really is good, and I had such a fun time doing it.

If you haven't watched it, check it out. I think you'll enjoy it.

25 CREED

A lot of people have heard the legend of when Sylvester Stallone sold his dog because he was so broke. The internet version is stretched some, but Sly did sell his dog, Butkus, to a guy outside of a 7-Eleven. After he sold the *Rocky* script, he bought Butkus back for much more ($15,000 in the internet version), and then put him in the movie.

The other legend is that Sly pitched the script and had interest from studios, but they wanted a name actor to play the role of Rocky. He said that it was him or nobody, and took much less money. Again, I don't know how much this has been stretched, but I do know that Sly became inspired to write *Rocky* when he watched Muhammad Ali fight Chuck Wepner. Ali dominated, but Wepner stood his ground and fought with a ton of heart.

Think about it. Sylvester Stallone was inspired by that one moment, and that led to him writing *Rocky*. After that, he took all those steps to sell the script and became a star while being so broke that he had to sell his dog at one point. He then went on to become a megastar in one huge movie after another.

Sylvester Stallone embodies the never quit spirit that we all have, but very few actually release it and achieve greatness. Maybe because of fear or laziness or because we've been told we didn't have it in us. I'd always had great respect for Sly, and I've tried to live with that never quit spirit.

And then I was offered a part in *Rocky Balboa*. At the time I had boxing matches scheduled in London. I told Charlotte about it, and that I'd have to turn it down despite my desire to take the role. I had commitments.

"Are you crazy?" she asked. "Rocky is an American icon. You have to do it."

She was right, as usual, and thankfully I jumped at the opportunity (I talk about this in depth in my first book). It was very cool being in *Rocky Balboa*, and it led to the opportunity to be in *Creed*.

Creed came about when I was at the WBC in Las Vegas. I was walking into the auditorium when I saw Jack Reiss. "Hey Stitch, they're trying to get hold of you to do a movie," he said. "Would you mind if I give them your number?"

"Yeah, please give them my number," I replied.

Five minutes later, I got a call from Robert Sally. He's one of the stunt coordinators. He told me that they would like to have me in the movie. I of course said I was in.

The production company called me with specifics, and once again I was flying out to the east coast to do a movie. This time I'd be in Philadelphia for six weeks.

I arrived a day before I was scheduled to shoot so I could meet everyone. I was taken to wardrobe where I got fitted for my outfits. They pretty much looked like the same clothes I had on. I also went to makeup where I would spend every morning getting styled for the day.

On the set Andre and Michael were practicing their fight scene.

When they finished, Andre saw me and gave me a hug. We talked briefly, and then I saw a young guy standing across the room with his hat on sideways and his jeans sagging below his butt. I'm kind of old school when it comes to clothes. I always iron my shirts and pants and try to present myself in a respectable way.

I walked toward him with the idea that I was going to tell him he should pull his pants up. As I got close, he turned and saw me coming. "Hey, Stitch! How are you doing? I'm Ryan Coogler, the director."

"It's great to meet you," I said, as I decided that he could wear his pants however he wanted.

Ryan is from Oakland. He wrote and directed Fruitvale Station, an absolutely awesome movie that Michael B. Jordan starred in. During that time Ryan was talking with Andre Ward about a cutman. Andre said, "Look, you have to get Stitch. There's nobody better."

But originally they were going to use the incredible actor Luis Guzman as the cutman. He's been in over a hundred movies and has to be one of the best character actors in the business. Everybody knows his face. For some reason they decided to go with me.

During my first scene Adonis was fighting Leo Sporino, played by Gabe Rosado. They did that whole scene in one shot. Adonis got cut, so after the first round I went in to work on it. They gave the ten-second warning, and it was time for us to leave. As Adonis stood, he brought his left arm over the rope and popped me right in the eye so hard that it knocked the lens out of my glasses. I spent the next couple minutes frantically struggling to get the lens back in while blinking my eye.

"Oh crap, what a way to start," I thought to myself.

When I woke up the next morning my eye was pretty sore. I looked in the mirror, and it was black!

When I got to the trailer, I saw Michael B. Jordan. "Michael, come here," I said. "I've got a bone to pick with you."

I showed him my eye and he said, "Oh, man. I'm so sorry."

I laughed. "It's all good. I understand."

I showed it to the people at makeup, and they thought it was perfect and wanted to leave it as it was.

I took a couple pictures with Michael with him pointing to my eye. It was pretty funny.

I have to mention Ricardo "Padman" McGill. He's an actual trainer from Philadelphia, and when Ryan Coogler was scouting locations he went to his First Street Gym where we ended up doing the gym work. He saw Padman doing pads, and he was so impressed he brought him onboard.

Padman is about as naïve as they come when it comes to Hollywood. Before we were to shoot the big fight against "Pretty" Ricky Conlan, played by Tony Bellew, we were standing in the center of the ring in the auditorium and all the walls were green. There were seats for maybe a thousand people.

"You know, Padman, during the movie there's going to be 70,000 people here."

He looked at me in disbelief. "How are they going to do that?"

I had to explain the green screen and movie magic.

Padman became everyone's favorite. He was THE guy. I told Ryan Coogler that he couldn't have picked a better guy to represent a Philadelphia gym.

I got to spend every day with Michael B. Jordan in his dressing room as I wrapped his hands. We got that one on one time, and what a tremendous kid. As an actor, he turned out to be a great athlete. During the end of our fifth week I was in his trailer, and I said, "Look, I have to knight you as a fighter because of the work you have done. You have represented this sport as well as any actor ever has. Not only for boxing, but for yourself. I'm going to knight you as a fighter."

He gave me a big hug and told me he loved me. He really appreciated it, and it wasn't an empty compliment. He really did such a tremendous job as a boxer.

Of course, he wasn't the only one to shine. The guy who

started it all after selling his dog was incredible as well.

26 ROCKY

When I was in *Rocky Balboa* I worked in Antonio Tarver's corner, so I got to see Sylvester Stallone work not only as a writer and a director, but as an actor. During that week I noticed how much of a genius he was, so when I got the call to work with him I was beyond stoked.

However, when I got the script my name was Marcel. I didn't like it, and every time I told somebody that my name would be Marcel, they laughed. I had to figure out how to change that.

Luckily, I didn't have to. During the scene when we meet Adonis in the gym, Rocky comes in and introduces us. He said, "…and Stitch, the best cutman in Philadelphia. Hope we don't need him."

I got chills throughout my body and I'm thinking, "YES! YES!"

I mean even though Ryan Coogler wrote and directed the movie, who is going to tell Sylvester Stallone that he can't call me Stitch?

The next day when we were filming I got up on the apron next to Sly. "Look, Sly. I want to thank you personally for using my name yesterday."

"It couldn't have happened any other way," he said. "It had to happen this way."

"I really appreciate it," I said.

Sly was real calm about it. He's not arrogant. He's definitely confident, but not arrogant. He's very much a team player, and he realizes the importance of making each scene as realistic as possible.

I watched him closely and tried to learn a lot from him when it came to acting. What he did most of the time was just gym talk. A lot of what he said in the movie wasn't even scripted. It just popped out of his head.

I tried to follow that style and stay nice and relaxed while I just pretended we were in the gym. As it was happening, I kept thinking that I couldn't believe I was part of Rocky's team.

It was about as awesome as it can get for someone in my position as a cutman. I was fortunate enough to have the opportunity to work with Sylvester Stallone in two Rocky movies. It's still hard to believe.

Sly is great with his one-liners because he's so quick-witted. During one of the breaks we were sitting with the makeup people, and one of Sly's assistants was there. He was talking about me to them. "This is Stitch. He's the best cutman in the business. And he looks like Edward James Olmos."

Stallone was standing there with his arms crossed, and without skipping a beat he said, "Huh, more like Edward James Almost," and then walked away with a smirk.

Damn, Sly just busted on me, but what could I say! It was hilarious the way he did it, and I couldn't help but laugh.

We did so much great work for that movie. I just knew it would be sensational.

Charlotte, and my son Daniel, and I went to the premiere, and wow. We had the red carpet treatment and got to see the movie. Arnold Schwarzenegger was sitting in front of me. Dolph Lundgren, Carl Weathers, all the old cast was there. Then we had the after-premiere party. Everybody was talking about how great the movie was.

They loved the part with my fingers on the neck. I won't say anymore because I don't want to give anything away in case you haven't seen it, but that was a creation of Ryan Coogler. It was brilliant, and during the premiere when I did that the whole audience started clapping.

At the party, Wesley Snipes came up to me. The first thing to come out of his mouth wasn't about the movie. He said, "Man, the UFC did you wrong."

It was really awesome to know that people of this magnitude, people like Wesley Snipes, supported me. And so many people still believed in me.

When I see Wesley Snipes again I'll be sure to tell him how much those words meant to me. It shows that many people believe I did the right thing.

After being told that I wouldn't work for the UFC anymore, I was heartbroken, but I pulled myself up and moved forward while taking every opportunity I could to apply my never quit spirit. And I didn't even have to sell my dog to do it.

27 LATIN LEGENDS

As you know from the name of my book, my goal was to make it to Madison Square Garden in New York City. I eventually did make it, but I never expected the dream to continue as it has. In this story, I went from The Garden, back to the fields.

At the time, New York still hadn't legalized MMA, so the UFC held their shows at the Prudential Center in Newark.

Going back to the East Coast had another special meaning because I had made friends with Adam Scherzer and Ricardo "Padman" McGill during the filming of *Creed*. Adam was our agent during the filming and made sure we had everything we needed. Padman of course was part of the Adonis team.

Filming had finished three weeks earlier. We were still pumped to have been part of this incredible movie. Philadelphia was a short drive so they decided to come to Newark and hang out for the day.

Throughout my career I have met some of the most interesting people who have become part of my life. Adam and Padman are two such people. There is definitely something to be said for being open and willing to meet others and welcome them into your life.

The main event in Newark featured Lyoto Machida against Luke Rockhold. During the Max Holloway and Cub Swanson fight I got a glimpse of actor Luis Guzman sitting ringside. Outside of being a fan, I had a special interest to meet him. As I mentioned, when I got the call to be in the *Creed* movie I googled the cast. Luis Guzman appeared as the cutman. I thought I was going to have to audition for the part. That never happened.

I introduced myself to him. We chatted, and then he asked his manager to take a picture of us. Of course, I also wanted a picture of Luis and me.

Who would have known that this would be the start of something special?

After the show, Adam, Padman, and I were sitting outside of my hotel relaxing and catching up. An SUV drove up and Jeff Wynne, a UFC employee who handles the sales of all shirts and caps, jumped out. He asked me if I would be willing to take a photo with his friend.

Never missing an opportunity like that, I said, "Yes."

Jeff's friend happened to be Ed Martin, manager of Luis Guzman. He is the one who took the photos of Luis and me at ringside. We hit it off like best of friends and chatted outside the hotel for the next two hours.

It was fate, like the time Zac Robinson contacted me to write the first book when I was going to be in Germany (where he lives) two weeks later to work with Vitali Klitschko. Zac and I met, spent three days together, shook hands and wrote our first book.

The same thing happened with Ed and me. The week after the UFC show, Wladimir Klitschko was fighting Bryant Jennings at the Garden. I hooked up with Ed, and I definitely didn't expect the red carpet treatment that I received.

The Klitschko team was staying at the Waldorf Astoria, a magnificent and historical hotel. Ed and his partner, Marc Calixte, picked me up and we had dinner, then we met up with Eric Pagan, inspector for NYPD, at his favorite cigar bar.

This is when I actually found out who they were and all that they did. Inspector Eric Pagan is one of the highest ranking police officers in the NYPD. Ed was more than just Luis' manager. He's also a movie, TV, and music producer who has worked with many of the top artist and actors. Marc is the guy you go to when you want to make things happen. I was surrounded by the best of the best at what they do.

None of that made a difference. I was glad to be in New York City, and most important to be with good people. We had such a great time.

I was still in awe from my first night in NYC, and then Ed and Marc took me to the HBO headquarters where I met many of the top executives. I couldn't believe the people I was meeting, and it was even more shocking that they knew who I was.

Deep inside I wondered what this kid from Planada was doing at the HBO headquarters in New York City meeting all these people.

The following day, Wladimir was to defend his title against Jennings. We didn't have to report to The Garden until 6:00 pm. While lounging at the cigar bar the night before, Eric had invited Ed and me to go on patrol with him in Spanish Harlem. With time to kill, I gladly accepted. It was a once-in-a-lifetime experience.

Things only got better. Ed had been working on a project where he was producing a series of documentaries featuring some of the great Latin Legends. Actors Luis Guzman and Danny Trejo, Yankees pitcher, Mariano Rivera, music legend, Eddie Palmieri, and others. Roberto Duran was also on the list of possible legends.

Ed decided that he would forfeit one Duran for another, and asked me if I would be interested in being part of his series of documentaries.

Like the handshake Zac and I had, I was honored to even be considered. I reached out, grabbed Ed's hand, shook it and responded with a quick yes.

I sent Ed a copy of my first book so that he could get a grasp of my life.

With that, director Jean Shepard and Ed wrote the script. It was wonderful.

For the meat and potatoes of the documentary, Jean Shepard met me in Düsseldorf, Germany, where Wladimir was fighting Tyson Fury, the fight that changed the whole landscape of the heavyweight division.

He got in-depth interviews with Wladimir, Vitali and members of the Klitschko team. German cutman and friend, Michael Schmidt, was there as our translator and location scout.

The interviews and footage Jean got was remarkable, but it was nothing compared to what was to follow.

The day after Wladimir lost to Tyson Fury, and a commentator said, "Wladimir looked bad losing to a guy who looked worse," Jean and I flew to the Central Valley to film in my hometown of Planada and its surrounding areas.

After reading my book, Jean was interested in getting footage of the migrant camps where we grew up, canals where we swam, and some of the fields where we worked. He also wanted to interview some of the friends I grew up with.

Creed had come out nine days earlier, and Ed had a brilliant idea. He bought one hundred tickets so I could invite friends and family to see the movie together. I hadn't seen some of them in thirty or forty years. I reserved forty of the tickets for the Planada Boxing Club, a program I support that keeps the kids off the streets.

My brother Benny spoke to the theater manager and reserved a theater just for us. The school supplied a bus to transport the kids from Planada to the theater and back, a nine-mile trip. The script had taken shape, and everyone was excited to be part of this documentary.

After a long flight back from Germany, Jean and I rested during the day before meeting up with a group of friends in the evening for pizza. It was good seeing George Parga, Bobby Burrola, Danny Peters, David Zarate, Frankie Miranda, Ray Gonzalez, and Chulo.

Leonard Hosie made the long flight from Bismarck, North Dakota to show his support and joined us for the first day of filming.

We met at Chulo's house at six in the morning to get shots of the sun shining on the fields and canals, then we were off to the migrant camps. Next, we went to Planada Elementary School where we got footage of the kids training under coach, Lucy Lopez. After wrapping some of the kids' hands, we finished with me signing posters furnished by the production team of *Creed*.

Jean got four kids who would represent Chulo, Marcial, Noe, and me as young kids running in the fields and canals. Something we did often.

There was a buzz in the town, and the support I received from the parents and Principal Aldonso Nave made filming easy. Seeing these kids run in the fields and canal made me realize that we had natural obstacle courses, which helped us be athletic.

The theater manager had set up a table so that I could sign the remaining posters for my friends and family who attended.

The school bus pulled up to the front of the theater. The kids stepped off as if they were going to attend the premiere of *Creed*. There was so much positive energy from the reunion that we could have easily lit up the projector.

I sat with my family and felt the excitement around me as the movie played. The theater next to us probably heard the thunderous applause and cheering when Rocky introduced me to Adonis by saying, "This is Stitch, best cutman in Philadelphia."

It gave me chills.

Our final shot was a classic move when Jean gathered everyone outside the theater. A drone flew overhead, filming us as we waved goodbye.

Jean, Leonard, and I flew out the next morning. We knew that we had just accomplished something special. I cannot thank them enough for including me in the Latin Legends series. It was such an honor, and it meant so much for so many people from my hometown.

This really was a case of me going from the Garden to the fields, and it was just as much, if not more special than when I had finally made it to Madison Square Garden.

28 GIVING BACK

A s I was going out into the world outside of Planada I always dreamed of returning and doing something for the town and the people.

As I mentioned before, during the hot summers we would all go swimming and cool off in the canals. Along with baseball, it was our only means of summer recreation. The canals where always at full capacity in the summer time because that water was used to irrigate the crops. We swam at our own risk, many of us getting cut and scraped with the cement walls.

Our favorite hangout, Peter Deep, now has multiple signs saying, "NO SWIMMING."

Anyway, after leaving Planada I always dreamed of someday going back home and having a community swimming pool built by Lute's Market and the park. I would dedicate it to my father and call it, "The B.T Duran Community Pool."

That hasn't happened yet, but I have gone back and shared my success with the town.

Weeks before *Creed* finished filming, my brother Benny called me and said that the Merced County Sheriff and the School District were working together to build a boxing program at the school. The non-profit gym was created to keep the kids off the streets and away from drugs. The school turned a building into a gym. Amateur stand out Lucy Lopez is the head coach and the program is free to kids up to eighteen.

To get the program started they held a fundraiser for equipment and uniforms. Benny asked if I could attend and support the program. Of course I said yes.

Knowing what I know now and not having anything like this growing up, I wanted to make this a special event. I contacted Bad Boy owner, Robin Offner and asked him if he could help out. Without hesitation he said yes and sent the kids shirts, hand wraps, and equipment to kick off the program.

Since I'd developed a great relationship with the cast of *Creed*, Robin also sent me gloves to have the crew sign so that we could raffle them at the fundraiser. Sly, Michael B. Jordan, Andre Ward, Padman, Tony Bellow, director Ryan Coogler, and I signed the gloves

Wladimir Klitschko and camp manager David Williams also sent four signed gloves.

I arrived at the recently built Cesar Chavez Middle School and smiled with joy. It was nothing but a pasture when I was growing up, and it was across the road from where I had lived. The same road, Plainsburg, is where the school namesake and others walked on their way to Sacramento, the state capital, in protest of unfair working conditions for farm workers.

Arriving at the gym with Ralph, I saw my brother Benny, and Marcial and Noe standing next to a camera crew. The news channel had made the fifty-mile drive from Fresno to film the event.

The reporter asked me how I felt coming back home and being part of this program. I didn't think it was possible, but I choked! I started off confident in my answer, and then the emotions hit me. I had to stop the interview to compose myself. The feeling was overwhelming. I was home.

Photo: Planada

In the school gym I saw many of the elders and people I grew up with. The event was sold out.

The projected goal for the fundraiser was $10,000. With the support I received from Robin, the *Creed* team, and Wladimir, we destroyed the goal and reached $23,000. The kids will now be able to train, travel and have fun.

Other moments, like when Ed Martin, producer of Latin Legends, bought one hundred tickets so that I could invite friends, family and the boxing team to the screening of *Creed* is what giving back is all about.

Another time, Scott Coker was having a Bellator show in Fresno. Having continued to give back to Planada, I asked him if he would be willing to donate fifty tickets so that I could invite the boxing club and some of my friends who had never seen a live show. They would also get to see me work for the first time.

He was more than happy to participate. He smiled and said, "Gotta share Bellator love."

That he did!

Coach Lucy Lopez coordinated the trip, and the school district furnished a bus.

Alfred Taren and Fred Colbert, my sponsors, "The 86ers," created fifty Stitch shirts so that I could surprise the kids and my friends. What a powerful display of support. The black shirts with green lettering dominated section 113.

Photo: 86ers

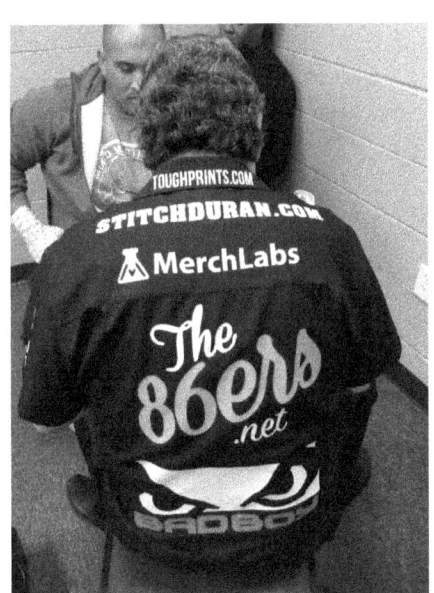

Moments like these are what keep me energized. I know that giving back can make a difference in someone's life.

I will continue to do anything I can for Planada and the boxing club. I won't be satisfied until we can all go swimming in the "B.T. Duran Community Pool."

PART 6:

SUPPORTING THE TROOPS

29 ON THE WAY TO AFGHANISTAN

This is a very special chapter for me because of the people I met and the things that I did. Throughout our time here we have maybe a dozen moments that are life changing. They give us a new perspective, open up a whole new world, make us consider how fortunate we are, or bring people into our lives that we know will always be a part of it for the rest of our days. My trip to Afghanistan was one of my life-changing moments, and it definitely sits on top of my bucket list of accomplishments.

As an honorary of the MMAJunkie Hall of Fame, I often co-host the show with George and Goze. If you don't listen to Junkie Radio, start. It's one of, if not the, best in the business. George and Goze invited me to be part of a tour they put together to support the troops in Afghanistan. This was an offer I could not refuse.

The group included: George and Goze, Steve Straub, our road manager who did a fantastic job keeping us on time, UFC fighters Amir Sadollah and Jake Ellenberger, and me. George, Goze, Steve, and I left Las Vegas to meet the rest of the team and we all hooked up with Sgt. Toney, our official Armed Forces Entertainment escort.

The trip from Chicago to Istanbul Turkey took eleven hours.

Jake, Amir and I were all accustomed to these long trips. George, Goze and Steve where still traveling rookies.

We landed in Istanbul, the only city where part of it is in Asia and the other part in Europe. Luckily, this was before all the recent chaos in Turkey.

We were all pretty tired, but didn't have much time before our final connection, a five-hour flight from Istanbul to Manas International Airport, Bishkek, Kyrgyzstan. We arrived at 3:00 am with a whopping thirteen-hour time difference from our home in Las Vegas. We basically lost a day while traveling.

Manas is a transit center and former US Military installation where the GIs go before they transfer to Afghanistan. It is also the final stop for the GIs coming home from their dangerous tours. It gives them a chance to decompress and relax. George Wallace was also on the flight with us. He's a comedian who has been in a handful of movies and was the best man at Jerry Seinfeld's wedding. He's a funny guy and I knew the troops would love listening to his act.

About a half dozen soldiers greeted us at the terminal. We breezed through customs, claimed our bags, and were off to the military base. George tried to take a picture of the sign that read, "Welcome to Kyrgyzstan," but was told that it would not be a good idea. It was a little moment where we realized how serious this was.

Once on base, we went to PERSCO for in-processing, received our keys to our rooms, and had a chance to rest and catch up on some much-needed sleep.

We were all starving when we awoke and had lunch with the troops in their dining hall. We chatted with the soldiers, many being huge MMA fans. They talked about the Wanderlei Silva/Rich Franklin fight, and the release of Rousimar Palhares from the UFC was also a big topic. We all gave our opinion of the upcoming Cain Velasquez/Junior Dos Santos fight. It would turn out to be a fight that we would watch with the soldiers on our return visit to Manas, from Afghanistan.

After a thirty-minute break they escorted us to the flight line to see all the military air power. I was in the Air Force a long time ago. Seeing all that our military has now is pretty awe-inspiring.

From there, we went to the K-9 unit where we all had a chance to put on our, "I'm going to get bit gear." Our attack dog was an intimidating Belgian Malinois named Lennox. Some of you may remember the story of Diesel, a heroic Belgian Malinois who was killed as he led an assault on the terrorists who masterminded the attacks on Paris in 2015. The raid resulted in the death of two terrorists and the apprehension of many others. After meeting Lennox, I'm sure Diesel ran into that house with courage in his heart even though he understood the danger. The breed isn't a particularly big dog, but they are strong, tough, intimidating, and as loyal as they come.

For some crazy reason I volunteered to be the first to try to run away from Lennox. I was fully padded down with my protective gear, but it still was not a good idea. Lennox tracked me down, clamped onto my elbow, and dragged me to the ground like a rag doll.

At that moment I just knew that I would be going home in a cast. The pain shot through my arm and up into my shoulder. It felt like my arm was being eaten, and I was wearing protective gear! But when his handler called him off he did exactly as he was supposed to do and stopped the attack. It is incredible how well the dogs and soldiers work together.

Goze was a real trooper and took one for the team. He took off running down the field with all that padding, and Lennox gave chase. In a matter of seconds he dragged Goze to the ground and pulled on his protective gear so hard that he almost pulled it off.

We all laughed so hard because as George put it, "He looked like a turtle with his top pulled over his head."

The release from Lennox came when Goze tapped out.

I feel sorry for those criminals or terrorist who get caught by these K-9 masters without this type of gear, but not too sorry.

After this crazy adventure, we had some down time. We sat outside of our dorms licking our wounds and laughing about our experience with Lennox.

We noticed that there was a large amount of soldiers from different parts of the world who were there as part of the coalition. We saw soldiers from Poland, Croatia, France, the UK, Australia, Mongolia and even small countries like El Salvador. I don't know exactly how many countries represented the coalition, but I do know we were in good hands.

At five in the evening we arrived at the fitness center for our first MMA clinic and a Meet and Greet.

About fifty participants showed up. George introduced all of us. Jake and Amir took over from there and worked with the soldiers on grappling and submission skills.

Bad Boy, who sponsors me, also designed and donated a bunch of shirts to give out to the troops. They became an instant hit.

After the training session and Q & A period, everyone was still full of adrenaline. We chose a couple participants and I wrapped their hands. The looks on their faces when they were getting wrapped showed that it was a special moment for all of us.

With little rest, we had dinner and then attended the George Wallace show. The soldiers are only entitled to two beers per night. In Afghanistan, drinking alcohol is prohibited. The returning GIs enjoyed every drop of their two beers. We also had our two beers as we chatted with the soldiers and watched the comedy show.

Even though George was hilarious, we were tired from our long trip, getting beaten up by Lennox, and then working out with the soldiers. We struggled to stay alert and enjoy the show. The soldiers had much more energy than we did.

As soon as it was over we went to bed and prepared for the next day.

30 DOWN RANGE GEAR

After breakfast we took a tour of Bishkek, the capital city of Kyrgyzstan. We had the opportunity to see the changing of the guard at one of their national monuments, and then we were off to the mall to do some local shopping.

Upon returning, we met with a colonel who briefed us about the base, our tour, and our next stops (classified for now).

Photo: Flak Jackets

The reality of being in a combat zone soon hit us as we were fitted with, "Down Range Gear," which consisted of a flak vest with heavy metal plates and a helmet. We all looked at each other like everything just got real, and we were a little more somber as we geared up.

The equipment is heavy. It is amazing that this type of gear is sometimes worn 24/7 for weeks—even months—at a time. Often the temperatures reach one hundred and twenty degrees or more, and yet the soldiers go out and do their jobs professionally despite the miserable conditions.

Our second clinic was also a success with just about as many soldiers participating as the day before.

Amir and Jake took control and went over some warm up exercises and then started with grappling and striking drills. George, Goze, and I did some pad work with others.

I saw a soldier who had great kickboxing skills. I told him I'd work the pads for him. His kicks and punches popped the pads and echoed throughout the gym. We worked out for five rounds and I built up a nice sweat. It reminded me of those days so long ago when I spent all day every day with kickboxing and padded out Dennis Alexio and many other great kickboxers.

George, through his daily blog said it best, "It was great to see Stitch take that role that we were unfamiliar with, him holding pads. See, we often catch Stitch tending to cuts and bruises during the fights and we know that he's a great hand wrapper. But a great cornerman can also get you warmed up properly, and Stitch has been doing that for years. It's just that we don't see much of that because we mostly catch him during the broadcast of the events we're watching."

It was a nice compliment, and it made me feel proud, but those words would soon bite me in the ass!

After the work out, we showered and walked to the chow hall where we ate with the troops and shared stories.

Since we were flying to Afghanistan the following day, we returned to our rooms, packed our bags, and relaxed.

Steve Straub and Sgt. Toney had given us a report time of 12:00 am with a departure time of 4:00.

In preparation for our departure we had to put on our flak vest and helmet and walk to the terminal in the cold weather.

When I was younger, I'd been a trainer in kickboxing and boxing for many years, but it had been a while since I padded someone out like I'd done the day before. I tried to put my vest on and found out quickly that my arms and shoulders had locked up on me from holding pads for this strong kickboxer. I could not lift my arms over my head to put my vest on. Was I getting old or just out of shape? Probably a combination of both.

One thing I hadn't lost was my ability to think quickly and adapt when needed. I painfully tossed the vest on the top bunk bed and squeezed my head and body into place. I felt like a Komodo dragon ramming his head into a dead carcass while ripping away at my flak vest. After a whole lot of struggle, I did it. Mission accomplished!

Once we arrived at the terminal, we were on complete lockdown. After sitting patiently for an hour, our flight was delayed until 6:30. We went back to our quarters and returned at four for our new departure time.

We marched to the C-17 on the flight line and got on board. Our route to Afghanistan was to go over the Himalayas, and we had a chance to sit in the cockpit with the pilots. Goze and I went first and the view was remarkable.

Amir and Steve had a butt-clinching moment during their visit in the cockpit. Flying over hostile territory, the C-17 defense system detected a "missile lock" and set off an alarm. The pilots must have noticed their reaction and quickly let them know that everything was okay.

We landed in Bagram Air Base and were met by our liaison Mr. Bierman and Capt. Jenkins, the officer assigned to look after us. Keep in mind, we came under "general status" and would have bodyguards 24/7.

After breakfast we met with General McConnell, a two-star general who I would later see at the aforementioned Tim Kennedy fight. He briefed us and also said his son was a big MMA fan. During the briefing, the war in Afghanistan became real. The general received a phone call. The Taliban had killed a governor from one of the provinces. It didn't seem to surprise him at all. We just sat there, not knowing what to say or how to react.

It was something of a sobering moment for me. Of course I knew that people were killed here all too often, but to hear it and recognize that it wasn't even a surprise really hit home. We were in a war zone, and nothing is a certainty there, not even being able to wake up to another sunrise.

31 BAD MOFOS

After spending time with General McConnell, we got to meet the Special Forces. We were amped. They are the valiant group that heads into the villages of Afghanistan to protect villagers and work in conjunction with the Afghan military. In other words, these are the baddest mofos in the military.

Once we got to the compound, we met this very big intimidating soldier in civilian clothes. His rugged face was covered in a thick red beard, and a beat up cap rested on his head. I'm sure that cap had its own stories to tell. He was introduced to us as "Silverback," and I could see why! He escorted us to the gym where we would meet the troops.

When we arrived at the gym he told us that the facility was named after SSGT Gene Vance, a Special Forces Linguist from West Virginia who was killed, "In an intense fire fight while on patrol."

It gave me chills similar to the ones I got when I saw the movie Lone Survivor a few months after the tour. We civilians have no idea what these warriors go through on a daily basis. God Bless them!

As we were about to enter the room, Silverback, AKA Jim

Mahurin, looked at me and said in his deep southern voice, "Stitch, my wife loves you, and I love you!"

What a wonderful feeling. Not that they loved me, yes of course that meant a lot, but that he was an American hero and on our side. After we talked for a while I learned that this was Jim's seventh tour. It blew my mind that he'd done this seven times. I asked him why. He shrugged. "Brotherhood."

It was such a simple reply that carried such profound meaning.

It turned out that he is a big MMA fan, and he and his wife are both marital artists. We have now adopted him as part of the MMAJunkie family.

The training session soon began, and as always Jake and Amir broke sweat training and instructing these badass guys. After our Q & A session, I wanted to take a photo with the troops. Since everyone carried weapons 24/7, I asked this one soldier if I could hold his rifle. He told me to wait just a minute. He hurried off to his barracks and came back with an AK-47.

With confidence that was bordering on cockiness, he said that he had gotten the weapon from a dead Taliban. Imagine what went through my mind as I was taking this photo. I have a whole new respect for the Special Forces. They are some bad mofos!

After wrapping Silverback, and then Lieutenant Colonel Moses' hands, we were presented with individual awards and a flag for being there and supporting the troops.

Throughout the trip we did seven or eight clinics and meet and greets. Every time we reached our destination we were informed on the safety factors and in the event of an attack where we would need to go and what we would need to do. Bunkers were everywhere. The day before we arrived, the base had received something like thirteen incoming mortars. One evening Jake and I got a little ballsy and stayed outside our rooms. We stared into the distance and talked in hushed tones. It was like we were saying we aren't afraid of you, but at the same time we stayed close to the bunkers just in case the mortars came. Thankfully, that never happened.

AFE had scheduled us to destinations that the average entertainer would not go to.

One of those trips was Camp Morehead, a base for the Commandos. Another group of badasses. It wasn't long after we left when apparent members of ISIL attacked, killing hundreds, burning homes, and beheading family members of local police officers. The commandos, some of the same ones I'm sure we met, were inserted by helicopter. Not long after that it was reported that the immediate threat had been nullified.

As we flew to Camp Morehead in two Blackhawks fully loaded with gunners, ammo, and our bodyguards, Jake, Amir, Goze, George, Steve and I listened to the turning of the chopper blades as we looked down at the villages. We understood that we could be targeted at any time.

Fully-armed soldiers were stationed outside waiting for our arrival. Once the choppers landed, we were immediately escorted to the compound where we would spend time with these professional killers.

The reality of combat set in when Goze and I watched a couple commandos body search a group of Afghan soldiers who wanted to meet us. These guys where working side by side with the American forces, and yet the chances of them having explosive devices was still a possibility.

Again, I considered where I was. It was both exhilarating and scary, and I'm so glad I made this trip. The way I saw it was that we were able to provide a little bit of a distraction from the overwhelming grind of war. The soldiers appreciated it, and often thanked us for coming to visit them. We replied by thanking them right back. All of us were humbled as we met so many men willing to risk their lives for their country.

32 KILLER

We made our way through Camp Morehead and chatted with almost everyone there. One young man asked me if I ever heard of Danny "Little Red" Lopez, WBC Featherweight champion. Of course I had. "He was a great Latin fighter in the '70s and '80s," I said.

Turns out, Danny Lopez was his grandfather. I could see the pride in his eyes knowing that I remembered him. Moments like these are what made our tour special because we were able to give these American Heroes some positive memories.

Another great story while in Bagram happened at the chow hall. I was sitting next to a soldier from Poland. He said, "Stitch, you know, I studied Brazilian jujitsu and that has given me the calming effect to accept death. As I hear these bullets buzzing by me, I tell myself, if I go, I am taking you with me."

Strong words from a soldier that was there as part of the coalition. I was mesmerized by his comment. What mental strength these soldiers have to have in order to survive in the battlefield.

Another time, Amir, Jake and I were walking around the market on base. A soldier from Croatia recognized us and wanted to take a photo. We took one, and then he turned to Jake and

Amir, "No offense to you guys, but I want to take a picture with Stitch."

I guess he recognized me wrapping the hands and working the corners of Mirko "Cro Cop" Filipovic, the famous MMA fighter from his home country. As we had our arms around each other and ready for a photo, he glanced up at me and said, "I'm not a fighter. I'm a killer."

I believed him. These soldiers deal with life and death on a regular basis.

Photo: Afghanistan

By the end of the tour we were all feeling quite important as we flew from base to base in Blackhawks. Our next visit was NKC, which is the home to ISAF. ISAF is a NATO-led security mission. I felt like I was in the movie Blackhawk Down as we closed in on our destination. The compound is located in Kabul. Once again, we flew over the area and I kept my eyes open looking for any unusual movement. I did have the complete confidence in the gunners, but I couldn't keep myself from scanning the ground.

Our scheduled landing was in the center of a soccer field, and there was a game going on as the choppers approached. The athletes ran to a safe place before the two Blackhawks landed and blew dust everywhere.

When we approached the field, armed guards rushed to their positions and ushered us into a safe place where we would meet and greet with soldiers who came to support us.

I'd wrapped so many hands by now, but I saved enough tape and gauze to wrap the hands of a couple soldiers who had covered our backs throughout the tour. It was my way of showing them my respect and appreciation for taking care of us.

One was Major Hood, a man who took pride in his uniform and was the one who made things happen for us. He always kept a stern face, so I made it my goal to make him smile. I gave him the knockout wrap, and we posed for a picture with both of us smiling.

Working with so many fighters in the past, I have learned how to read their eyes. Eyes say everything! Sergeant Perkins was one of these fighters. He'd been with us during the whole tour. He had seen me wrap dozens of soldiers' hands. He walked up to me with his M-16 hanging over his shoulder. "Can I ask you a question," he sheepishly asked.

I knew what he wanted and beat him to the punch. I stopped him in the middle of his question. "I would be honored to wrap your hands."

I did wrap his hands, and this became one of those special memories from my trip. These two soldiers gave us everything they had and that was a small way for me to thank them.

We finished the stay at ISAF when the staff ran flags up the pole. Each flag was used during a combat mission. Together, we folded them in military style and then they were gifted to us as a token of their appreciation.

It was such an honor to receive the flags.

The Blackhawks had arrived earlier than scheduled to pick us up and take us back to Bagram. The fear of being parked too long in the middle of the soccer field was a major concern because of incoming mortars. We had to cut our tour short and rush to the two Blackhawks.

As we ran towards the choppers, it was dark and all the lights were off. Despite being there for over a week, from time to time I still slipped into civilian mode. We strapped in, and during the lift off I decided I wanted to take a photo of the gunner manning his 50-caliber machine gun. I realized that our tour was basically over, and I think a part of me wanted to hold onto it. I gave it no thought and made a huge mistake by taking the photo. Both gunners had their night vision goggles on. The flash screwed up their night vision. Though I could not see his eyes, his body language said it all.

The lights were off because of the fear of having incoming directed at the two choppers. At that moment I recognized what a dumb thing I just did. I'd screwed up their vision for a few moments, and even worse, I could have given our position away. With my headphones on and listening to Santana, I just sat there like a little kid, punished for screwing up. Thankfully, we were able to fly out of there without incident.

33 EXPLOSION

Another incredible part of our trip was when we got to meet USMC four-star General Joseph "Fighting Joe" Dunford who at the time was Commandant of the Marine Corps International Security Force. As of writing, he is Chairman of the Joint Chief of Staff. You don't get much higher than that.

He was at Camp Phoenix for a ceremony where the base was changing hands from one General to another. Security was extremely high because of all the dignitaries present. I could see guards on rooftops and around the perimeter of the event.

After the ceremony, we were invited to meet the General. At the party, there was a long line of officers waiting to meet him. We picked a place to wait, loaded our plates with food, and chatted with some of the guests.

Soon we were escorted to the front of the line where we met and talked to General Dunford. Our presence there meant so much to the troops' morale that the General thanked us personally for taking the time to visit. We finished by taking pictures with him and many others.

During our three-day stay at Camp Phoenix, we had a chance to relax a bit, see the base, and spend time with the troops. Goze also managed to get enough of a strong signal to host MMAJunkie live. I'm sure it's the only MMA show to ever be live from Camp Phoenix.

On our last day in Bagram, we had some free time. While Jake was shopping at the market by the entrance to the base, there was a huge car explosion. Jake ran back to meet with us near the bunkers, and said he felt the blast and the tin roofs of the market were shaking and rattling.

Sergeant Perkins and his team immediately assembled. They were the first responders and quickly reported to the scene. It turned out that the explosion had killed something like ten people. It doesn't make sense to me. One moment people are walking around shopping, and the next they are killed in an explosion. It just isn't fair.

We were relieved to see the team come back safe. We asked Sergeant Perkins what happened. He simply replied with, "The Special Forces have neutralized the situation."

I don't know what that exactly meant, but knowing the capability of the Special Forces I understood that it didn't look good for the bad guys.

We had met some wonderful people on our tour, and our sendoff was an unexpected surprise. A group of supporters that we had hung out with had set up a festive area leading up to the flight line with lights and music. They had learned that I was a big Santana fan, so they had his music playing in the background. We hugged everyone that came to say good-bye and thanked them for having such a wonderful time.

With flak vest and helmets on, we boarded the C-17 with hundreds of soldiers who had finished their tours in Afghanistan, and headed back to Manas. We were proud to be flying home with these heroes and looking forward to our two beers and watching the Cain Velasquez/Junior Dos Santos fight with them.

We all assembled at the main Rec Center/bar to see the fights.

It was a festive night as the soldiers enjoyed their two beers.

UFC 166 was held at the Toyota Center in Houston, Texas, and transmitted to all the Armed Forces worldwide. What a night of fights. The one that stole the show was Gilbert Melendez vs. Diego Sanchez. I'd worked with both fighters, so I knew it was going to be a barnburner, and it was. Gilbert won the decision in an all-out battle. After that, Daniel Cormier took a decision over Roy Nelson setting up the main event.

That fight left no question that Cain Velasquez was indeed a true Mexican warrior. He stopped Dos Santos in a grueling fight that had Cain connecting on 274 total strikes to Junior's 62. The punishment that Dos Santos took was hard to watch as his face turned into a swollen mess.

It was a huge win for Cain, as it was almost two years earlier when dos Santos had taken the belt from him at Fox's debut event in Anaheim.

It was a high-energy night that we finished by taking pictures with the soldiers. It was a nice way to end our trip.

After eleven days on tour, we would be returning home with a new respect for the men and women in uniform. They sacrifice their lives so that we can live in a free nation.

Months later, our newfound friend and now brother, Jim "Silverback" Mahurin, attended our annual MMAJunkie gathering in Las Vegas. With approval from Lieutenant Colonel Moses, he surprised George, Goze, and I with a (CIB) Combat Infantryman's Badge that is worn by soldiers who have seen combat. In front of all the MMAJunkie family, we proudly received our pins. Along with my Autism pin, I proudly wear my CIB pin on my cornerman jacket in honor of the men and women we met and all the men and women who fight for our country.

34 ARMED FORCES ENTERTAINMENT

A got a call to go on a two-week long AFE tour to visit the troops stationed throughout Europe. After having such an incredible experience in Afghanistan, I jumped at the opportunity. The characters and the location had changed. It was almost like a vacation compared to Afghanistan, where we had bodyguards 24/7 and spent our time flying around in Blackhawks, but it was another memorable experience, and the group of guys I was with were a blast.

The others on the tour were Cole Escovedo, Frank Trigg, Tim Kennedy, Marcus Davis, and Oliver Copp and Zac (my co-author). George DeGrella, the AFE European Director and man who put it together, was with us for a large portion as well. We arrived in June 2014, and had a big tour bus and our own driver, the driving machine Sebastian Gladrow. He drove that thing through all kinds of narrow roads in Europe and England.

I didn't really know Cole Escovedo going into the tour since I never got to work with him during his career. He was the inaugural World Extreme Cagefighting featherweight champ, and he fought in the UFC late in his career against all odds.

Cole lives in Fresno, right down the road from where I grew up. He had a tough upbringing that he details in his book,

Through the Cage Door, and I knew he was a tough person, but he had me laughing throughout the tour.

He's got a great never quit spirit, and even though he's been through so much in his life, he's such a friendly and fun person.

He stole the show for me when it came to having us laughing. We were at this tiny base in England for a seminar. We had a great turnout, and this little Airwoman had taken a liking to Cole. Afterward, we were at the one and only bar/restaurant on the base. They got us pizza and we were enjoying a couple of beers.

The Airwoman from earlier begged and begged for Cole to give her a leg kick. Finally, he relented. He lined it up, and she tensed. He blasted her in the thigh, bone on bone, thump! It was a solid kick, but he held back a little bit.

Her reaction, man it was hilarious. Her whole body kind of trembled and she tumbled to the floor. We were all dying laughing. Cole helped her up, and as she rubbed her leg in pain there was a huge smile on her face.

We laughed and laughed about that moment for the rest of the trip.

I'd worked with Marcus Davis many times. Mark DellaGrotte used to train Marcus, and he'd call me off the record before his fights to ask if I'd wrap his hands and work his corner. I of course said I would every time.

One of the big lessons I learned with Marcus, that I pass on to others, is always prepare for the worst-case scenario. Marcus was always in great battles. This time it was against Chris Lytle. I had everything completely prepared even as the round was coming to an end. With about ten seconds left in the first round, Marcus got a bad cut. I was at the gate as the bell sounded.

I was able to keep him in the fight, and he went on to score a split decision and earn fight of the night honors.

Marcus could be an actual comedian. I'm serious. He had us laughing so hard. He said such off-the-wall things, and they were always perfectly timed. I'd love to share some of his jokes, especially the Uncle Marcus story, but I'd better leave it for him to tell. If you ever have the pleasure of meeting Marcus, ask him about it.

Aside from the fun times we had as we traveled, it was great to watch them work together as they taught the troops. You could see that they were passionate about it. They took no shortcuts and gave them their whole heart and soul. And at the end of each seminar I wrapped two or three people's hands. Everybody gathered around to watch and take pictures.

Listening to Tim Kennedy introducing everyone and talking to the troops was unbelievable. He is an inspirational guy. And Frank Trigg can get up and talk about anything at the drop of a hat.

I'd known Trigg better than anyone else. He was probably the most laid back in the group. He's got his crazy side for sure, but he didn't let it loose.

When we were in Mildenhall, England, there was a guy who had a 5-0 pro record and held a belt in a small promotion. He really wanted to go hard with Trigg to see what he was made of. I think he believed that he would be able to hang.

Trigg eased onto the mat, swinging his arms a bit to warm up his shoulders. He looked like an old man who'd just woken up. Then they slapped hands and boom, he took the guy down and submitted him in about forty-five seconds. They restarted, and Trigg tapped him again in under a minute. I'd say they rolled for about ten minutes and Trigg submitted him probably six times.

The guy couldn't believe it. He expected different results, and was pretty bummed about it. Trigg told him that he went hard to give him a real sense of self-awareness. Now he knew where he was and he understood how much he'd need to work to get where he wanted to be. I wish I had his name so I could see how his MMA career is progressing.

Tim was our unquestioned leader. I'd worked with him some, and I'd heard stories about what he'd done in the military, but to hear him talk about it was a whole different ballgame. It was great to see him work with guys who truly respected him as a great American hero.

I really got to see what Tim was made of during those two weeks. His interactions with the active duty soldiers were tremendous. He gave back in a different way than the rest of us. It just meant more to everyone to get to meet and talk with Tim.

We were at Ramstein Airbase in Germany, the largest base outside of the United States, at the hotel attached to the Base Exchange. We were walking inside and Tim saw a young muscled-up guy walking out. He turned and made a beeline straight towards him.

We all stopped in the lobby and waited. After a few minutes Tim returned. He asked Oliver, one of the tour managers, if the guy could join us for dinner. Oliver said it was fine.

Tim went on to explain that the guy was Special Forces and waiting for his flight to Afghanistan for his first tour. He was pretty nervous, so Tim wanted to talk to him and help put his mind at ease. Sure enough, he joined us for dinner at the Macaroni Grill and had a great time.

Throughout most of the tour, Tim didn't really drink. It's not like anybody was partying, but everybody would have a beer or two to wind down each day. I kept telling Tim that I was going to get him drunk. Finally, he said he'd have some drinks with me, but only if he could get some nice wine. We stopped in Lakenheath, England, and he picked up a couple bottles of nice Shiraz, and then we stopped in a small town and he ran off to find a cheese shop.

We opened the wine and toasted as the bus lumbered toward the English Channel. By the time we got on the ferry, we were both pretty tipsy. It was fun to see him let loose a little bit. I told him that it was my goal to get him a little messed up.

He laughed. "You did it, Stitch. You did it."

During the Bellator show in Austin, Texas, I saw him and his wife, Ginger. I was rehashing that story, and he looked at Ginger as a smile broke across his face. "He did!" he said to her.

I couldn't help but laugh thinking about such fun times.

Tim has seen the horrors of combat up close and personal. I remember a photo he showed us of a convoy of Taliban members. Next to each truck there was a person lying on the side of the road. His team of snipers had taken them out, preventing them from delivering a huge amount of weapons. They went back to front so they didn't alert the other drivers.

Despite all that Tim has been through, he is a well-adjusted and happy person. He is one hundred percent confident that he is doing what has to be done to protect our freedoms.

He is no doubt one of the most impressive and intelligent people I've ever been around.

Even though this tour was so much fun, we did meet many soldiers who had been through hell. Some of them were wounded badly and now have to deal with the pain every day for the rest of their lives. Our job was to give them just a little bit of a mental break from that, and we all took that job very seriously. If we could just give them a few moments where they could push it to the side and have fun, then we felt like we were providing them an invaluable service.

Lastly, I'd be remiss if I didn't mention hanging with Zac and Oliver and George. I've become friends with Zac and Oliver through the years, and it was great to get to experience visiting the troops with them. Oliver, the man in black, is reserved. He's also one of the classiest people I've ever met. He just has a way about him that exudes class. He did a great job ensuring that everything was organized and ran efficiently. He's one of those guys in the MMA world that everybody knows, and he knows a little something about everything. Before he got into the MMA world he was one of the German pro wrestling commentators and became well known through that.

We got lost in Ansbach, and it was great. We drove to the wrong Lakenheath in England, about four hours out of the way. Not so great. I wrapped an Irish bar owner's hands at Moloney's in downtown Kaiserslautern. And I met people like Rob Foster, a soldier who I still keep in contact with to this day.

If I ever have the opportunity to do another AFE tour through Europe, I won't hesitate. It was truly an honor.

PART 7:

THE REEBOK DEAL

35 THE MIDDLEMAN

Before getting into the Reebok deal I think it's important to provide some background on the work climate. Now I don't hold any malice toward the UFC, and I hope this doesn't come off as complaining. I'm just giving you information on how it was from the cutmen's perspective.

Prior to the Reebok deal, the UFC cutmen were getting no love from the UFC staff. We always joked that we were like Rudolph the Red-nose Reindeer. We never got invited to any Reindeer games.

We didn't asked for much. In fact, we seldom asked for anything. As Burt Watson would always say, "You guys do such a great job that you never get noticed."

That must have been the case, because nobody except for Burt ever met with us to see how the program was going. I guess that's a compliment when the bosses don't even need to check on you.

There is no question that we cutmen have contributed greatly to fighters winning fights and making extra money because of the work we did either wrapping their hands or controlling cuts and swelling.

The fans recognize that we play a role in giving them those extra rounds to enjoy. We get hugs, gratitude, and much appreciation from them regularly. It is these times that make our job worth it.

The fighters and trainers recognize it as well. Forrest Griffin sent me a card and a certificate to a nice restaurant for the work I did on him when he fought Shogun. After I wrapped Joe Stevenson's hands, he reached in his pocket and gave me something like thirty-seven dollars, probably all he had. I protested, but he insisted.

Amir Sadollah also showed his appreciation for my work by giving me a nice tip. Brock Lesnar, Shogun, Lyoto Machida, Tito, Vitor Belfort, Josh Barnett, and many more went the extra mile and gave me items from their team uniforms. I will always cherish those moments.

In all the years and hundreds of fights that I worked in the UFC, not once did anyone from the front office other than Jess and the UK guys notice what a good job we did, never a compliment or two, much less a bonus. We always remained the "unsung heroes," and we were okay with that because those who mattered, the fighters, coaches, and fans, recognized our importance. To make our jobs even tougher, we were assigned a middleman, a member of the staff that we had to go through for everything.

"Dana hired me to be the asshole," he once said. He took his job to heart, but it really wasn't necessary because we all worked hard to do the best we could for the fighters. We didn't need an asshole.

Keep in mind, this was the guy we reported to in the event we had any issues or questions.

He allowed me to use my Stitch Premium tape, and for about three months many of the cutmen used it. During a fight in Brazil, I was wrapping a fighter's hands when the middleman, who was making his dressing room checks, saw me and said, "What the f--- are you doing?"

This was in front of the fighters and trainers, and I couldn't believe it.

"You can't use that tape," he said. "Cover it up."

I was surprised by his aggressiveness, and said, "We've been using it for three months. What's the problem?"

He didn't answer. He just told me to cover it up. I did as he asked and put white tape over the Stitch Premium tape. Months later, guess who had their own branded tape?

When the UFC teamed up with Fox, any sponsors that represented ammo, knives, or guns, were not permitted to be advertised on their network. I had the Gun Store as one of my sponsors, and they were tremendous. We had a great relationship.

When I told our middleman that Chris, the owner of the Gun Store, was disappointed that nobody had contacted him about not being able to participate any longer, his quick and cold response was that Chris could suck his d---.

Strong words from a UFC representative that made me say, "Damn."

Don House and I worked the first World Series of Fighting in Las Vegas. Ray Sefo, president of WSOF and a good friend, called me and asked if I could get cutmen to work the show like we did in the UFC. "Of course," I said without giving it a second thought.

Our job is to keep these fighters safe, and as independent contractors it's also nice to make some extra cash.

Prior to WSOF, House and I worked every show that the UFC had scheduled. Afterward, we weren't scheduled to work the next five shows. We missed one in England and one in Tokyo.

I sent an e-mail to Dana's assistant and asked why we weren't working these shows. Her response in a nutshell was that they were going through tons of training with their "B" and "C" level cutmen to get them more used to events.

It made sense. The promotion was putting on more shows around the world and needed more cutmen, so I accepted the response. That is until I met with the middleman.

He responded by saying that we gave those guys credibility, meaning working with the WSOF, and then he said, "Let me put it to you this way. You are an independent contractor, and we hire you on a fight-by-fight basis."

Wow! Talk about feeling the wrath. I knew at that point that all of us were disposable in his eyes. Talk to any veteran cutman in the UFC and I'm sure they have a story or two to tell about their own experiences with the people we were supposed to report to.

And you know what, all of this was okay with us. We didn't exactly like it, but we could live with it. Everybody has their own management style and he chose to be harsh. I'm not angry with him in the least. I just don't think his style was necessary because all of us had followed our dreams and worked our way to the top of our profession. We love what we do and love taking care of the fighters. They are without a doubt the number one priority. I've gone out of my way to help fighters, and I've seen other cutmen do the same.

So yes, it sucked working for a guy who fancied himself as a tyrant, but we all dealt with it just fine.

Then the Reebok deal came along, and that changed the game forever.

36 GROWTH?

When I started with the UFC in 2001, my first sponsor was Tapout. Punk Ass, Skrape, and Mask were the trendsetters for all the companies that supported the fighters and cutmen.

Like everyone else, we all started at the bottom. The boys from Tapout literally sold t-shirts out of the trunks of their cars in the beginning. The exposure that they received from sponsoring fighters was the foundation for them becoming a worldwide brand.

Mask designed the vest that I wore for many years. It became so popular that fans would constantly offer to buy my outfit. The brilliant minds of the Tapout boys also created different outfits for me that I would sign and give to a fan after a UFC event. My friend, "Big John" McCarthy, was one of the lucky ones who received a vest. He had it hanging in his gym last time I was there.

The growth of the UFC also helped many of the companies grow with the exposure that the fighters and cutmen gave them during events and signings. Everybody was happy!

Eventually, the UFC decided to charge companies a tax in order to advertise during events. Tapout, BadBoy, Affliction, Team Punishment, One More Round, and many more paid the one hundred thousand dollars.

This was the standard for many years, and although the tax cut out some smaller companies, it seemed to work and everyone was happy with the program. UFC got paid to let companies advertise, companies got great exposure, and fighters and cutmen got paid to advertise their products.

Then the day came when we were told that the UFC had agreed to use Reebok as a sponsor and the fighters and cutmen could no longer use their sponsors during UFC events.

That came as a big blow because many of us were making more money with the sponsors than we were fighting or working a UFC event. The UFC had supported the sponsorship program for many years and helped build it knowing the benefits to the fighters and cutmen. Now that was coming to an end with us not having any say so on the new Reebok deal.

The beginning of the end was on August 31, 2013, at UFC 164 in Milwaukee. The UFC teamed up with Harley Davidson to promote the 110th anniversary for the biking icon.

The cutmen were told that we would have to wear a Harley Davidson patch on our uniforms. I sent an e-mail to our UFC liaison, (everything had to go through him) asking if we would be compensated for wearing the patch. His answer was a big fat no! Being team players, we wore the patches with no expectations, but looking back on it now it was a huge indicator of what was to come.

It was early December 2014, when the cutmen met with our liaison for a complimentary breakfast and meeting. It got off to a rocky start when the first words that came out of his mouth were, "I want you to know that my only interest is Zuffa, Frank, Lorenzo, and Dana."

Those words hit us like a ton of bricks. Our liaison was not there to support us, but to give us the bad news. He informed us that we would be losing our sponsors and would have to wear Reebok. This wouldn't have been such a terrible deal except for the last little bit. Not only would we be forced to wear Reebok, but also we would not even be compensated for it.

This was huge and terrible news. Many of us relied on our sponsorships in order to do what we loved. Now all of our sponsorship money would be taken away, leaving us with the much smaller amount that the UFC paid us per show.

No date was given for when the Reebok deal would take effect. We all assumed that it would be immediately, right before Christmas. Thankfully, that didn't happen. We had eight months before the hammer dropped on us.

During that stretch before the Reebok deal took effect, we tried to negotiate with our liaison about some form of compensation. The answer was always the same, "No money in the budget."

It was such a tough stretch. Charlotte and I had many long talks about what we would do when the Reebok deal began. We knew we'd be okay. I'd taken many risks throughout my life, and they were all integral in making me the man I am today. But it was a worrisome time.

The unveiling of the Reebok outfits sent the fans and many fighters into a frenzy. The media jumped on board as well, stating how much the fighters disliked the new outfits and pay scale. The fans hit social media with a majority of the comments being negative.

The entire Reebok deal was turning into a PR nightmare for the UFC, but it was much worse for us. It was putting our livelihoods at risk.

37 FIGHT WEEK

The first show that would be exclusively Reebok was UFC 189, Mendes vs. McGregor, July 11, 2015. This was a huge card during what has become "fight week" in Las Vegas each year in July. It's something of a week of celebration with the fan expo and about as many fight cards as the most avid fight fan can stand. I was all over the place at the expo, on Junkie Radio, working the Invicta Fights, you name it, and I was probably there. It's so great to interact with the fans and spend time taking photos with them and telling stories.

The MGM, and pretty much most of the strip, was overrun with the most insane Irish fans you've ever seen. Thousands of them had made the trip from Ireland to support McGregor. Originally, he was supposed to fight Jose Aldo, but Aldo was hurt so Mendes stepped in.

The fight just before Mendes and McGregor was the one that stole the show. Robbie Lawler and Rory McDonald went toe to toe and fought with pure heart and soul. It would look like one of them had the upper hand, and then the other would land a big shot. Both men were beaten and bloody fairly early in the fight.

Mike Afanasiev worked the corner of Rory McDonald, and I worked Robbie's corner. We all knew it had the potential to be a great fight, but as it started none of us thought it would turn into the fight of the year, if not the decade. These two warriors came to the corner bruised, bloodied, and banged up. Both Mike and I used every second possible to keep these fighters in the game and give them that "One More Round."

We were able to do this despite their busted up faces, and they went on to give the fans a show that they will not soon forget. It ended when Robbie was able to stop Rory early in the fifth round. What a fight!

My point to this story is that these are two "A" level athletes who were taken care of by two "A" level cutmen. Thanks to our abilities we were able to help give the fans one of the most exiting fights in UFC history and kept the fighters safe and healthy. Mike and I demonstrated that night how important we are to the fighters and how we can help change careers.

Prior to this epic fight and a really incredible night of fights, we arrived in our dressing room. We were given our Reebok shoes and a generic vest. I held mine up and looked at it and thought, "You have to be kidding."

The vest had "cutman" written on the right side and UFC on the other side, our names were on the back. No Reebok logo. We all came to the consensus that these things were generic and tacky.

I remembered how Mask designed my vest during those earlier days and how much the fans loved them. Nobody would be asking to buy this piece of crap, and it made me sad. There was a time when everybody involved in the sport ate, slept, and breathed mixed martial arts. Everybody was in it for the love of it. Sure they wanted to make money as well, but there was a pureness to the sport back then.

I don't think that Reebok fell in love with MMA so they wanted to be a part of it. They were in it for the money, and it was evident by the generic vest. At that point, when I held up that vest, I knew our lives had changed.

At the time I just couldn't have known how much my life was about to change and that this would be one of my last UFC shows.

38 SUPPORT

The UFC and Reebok received so much negative press surrounding UFC 189. It was one thing after another with fans and media bashing the deal. I talked with John Nash from Bloody Elbow the day after UFC 189, and in hindsight maybe it was not good timing because of the firestorm of negative publicity the deal had caused.

I have always been a fair and honest man when it came to speaking my mind. I never expected that this interview with John would create so much of a backlash that the ripple effects still continue to this day.

The questions that John asked where pertaining to the cutmen and how the Reebok deal would affect us. I answered them as honestly as I could and tried to be "politically correct."

The article went out July 20, 2015, and I instantly started receiving phone calls, text messages, e-mails, etc. from friends, fighters, trainers, referees, fans, commission members, and even UFC employees, supporting me for being the first one to speak out about the unfair practices surrounding this deal.

I was surprised that the article created that much excitement and anger. I just reported what had happened and explained why I thought it was unfair. Then after the interview I got the call that I talked about at the beginning of the book, the one from long-time friend and UFC executive, Marc Ratner. He broke the news that the UFC would no longer hire me.

When word got out, the fans went on social media and trashed Dana, the UFC, and Reebok, for releasing me the day after the article came out. The days and weeks after my release were unbelievable. That first week I did fifty-seven interviews worldwide and actually had camera crews coming to my house. The top Reddit discussion for the week had been my firing. This was big news!

So much had happened that it took a while for it to really sink in. I wouldn't be working with the UFC anymore. I hated this, because I'd been a part of the promotion for almost fifteen years. I was there as Dana and the Fertittas built it up. I was there for so many great fights and had the honor of playing an important role in a lot of them. Now it was over.

The following Monday on my way to co-host MMAJunkie with George and Goze at their studio in the Mandalay Bay, I was sitting in the back seat catching up on all the messages I was receiving. My son Daniel was driving, and my wife Charlotte was sitting in the passenger front seat.

Robin Offner, owner of Bad Boy and my sponsor, called me. I put the speakerphone on so my wife and son could hear. Robin, being the true giant that he is, said, "We would like to help you out. What if Bad Boy makes a shirt that resembles your cornerman jacket? We'll sell it and all the proceeds go to you for the next six months."

That instantly brought tears to our eyes. The love and support I was getting worldwide was unbelievable. I couldn't thank Robin enough for such a kind act.

Robby LeBlanc, a friend who does a segment on Facebook called "Motivator Monday," used my firing as his motivational speech for that day. I was going through my messages when I decided to hear his words. His message was so powerful and it couldn't have come at a better time. When I heard it I burst into tears once again.

Charlotte walked in just as I started to cry. She had a concerned look on her face and asked me what was wrong. Without saying a word I showed her Robby's message. She had tears in her eyes as well, and then she gave me a big hug. At that moment I knew I had done the right thing.

The tears that spilled down my cheeks weren't from sadness. They were a result of all the positive support I had been receiving. Robby reinforced my belief that what I did was correct, even if it meant leaving a great organization like the UFC.

Here is the link to Robby's Motivator Monday:

http://tinyurl.com/MotivatorMonday

My seven brothers and sisters were proud of me for sticking up for my rights. We all had been through struggles like this before as we grew up as migrant workers in the fields of the central valley.

As a young kid, I remember my father and mother supporting the United Farm Workers when Cesar Chavez led a group of protesters on a walk from Delano to our state capital. The 260-mile walk gained momentum and garnered the attention of a nationwide, and even worldwide, audience. The support grew as Chavez and many others passed through towns like Planada. It was the march for equal and fair treatment of farm workers, and it meant a lot to a lot of people. The farm workers made many sacrifices leading up to the march, believing that by sticking together they would be able to overcome.

I felt like in some ways I had represented all the fighters and cutmen on such a sensitive issue. They could not speak out or they may have been dealt with the same way that I was.

It was a terrible time for me, but oddly enough it is one of my proudest moments. A big reason for that is because of the outpouring of support from people all over the world. Cesar Chavez once said, "You are never strong enough that you don't need help."

I tried to be strong and do what I believed was right. I got a lot of help after the fact, and it was definitely needed and appreciated from the bottom of my heart.

My mother had passed away a year before UFC 189. She was such a strong woman and had done so much for me. I know she would have been proud of my stance for fairness. I felt like the Cesar Chavez of MMA.

PART 8:

A NEW BEGINNING

39 WSOF AND BELLATOR

The week following the release of the Bloody Elbow article and my release from the UFC was such a whirlwind. I knew that I needed to move on and start working somewhere else, but I barely had time to exhale as I did one interview after another and responded to hundreds of messages of support.

One of the first messages I received was from Ray Sefo. For those of you who don't know. Ray is from New Zealand and a world champion kickboxer. He also boxed and had a few MMA fights, and he's the president of The World Series of Fighting.

"Hey, Stitch," Ray said, "we're having a show soon and if you're interested we'd love to have you aboard."

I thought that was very admirable, because it was his first show with WSOF when we got suspended for working with him. When that happened, I had to tell him that we couldn't work anymore of his shows. I felt bad in doing so. Ray has been a good friend for many years.

I told him that I'd be glad to be a part of the show. I didn't even talk about dollars or cents. I felt like I owed him because I'd never had the opportunity to help WSOF like I'd wanted to.

WS22 was on August 1 at Planet Hollywood in Las Vegas.

The main event featured Jake Shields and Rousimar Palhares. Ray decided to have an autograph signing at the Fight Shop for me and Rousimar and Jake. They printed up cards for me to sign and pumped it up to the fans. It was really nice to be back working without skipping a beat.

So many fans showed up to meet me and take pictures, and they were overwhelmingly supportive. In the previous two weeks I'd felt like I'd been pulled in about a thousand different directions, and I'd been riding a rollercoaster of emotions.

Getting back to doing what I love and working with the fighters was such a relief. I couldn't help but think of so many moments in my past when I'd taken a big risk. I remembered that time in Planada when I was just out of high school. My friend and I were going to join the Air Force. He decided not to go at the last moment. I had a decision to make, and I decided to go.

Then there was the opening of my kickboxing school, American School of Kickboxing. I had to use credit cards to get the door open, but I believed in myself. The job offer for Vegas, complete with a huge pay cut, came not long after ASK opened. Again, we decided to take the risk. It of course paid off in a huge way.

All those moments, and many more, had gotten me to where I was. It had been so difficult when I was notified that the UFC wouldn't use me anymore. But the support I received told me I did the right thing.

As I sat there signing autographs and taking pictures with fans, I had an overwhelming sense of gratitude for everything that had happened, both good and bad.

About seven months before WS22, a couple weeks after Burt Watson had left the UFC, I gave Scott Coker a call. With the impending Reebok deal I decided that it would make sense to look for options. I asked Scott how he would like to have Burt and me on his Bellator team.

He wanted to meet with us, so we flew out to Santa Monica and met Scott in a hotel to talk about the possibility. It was great to sit and talk with him because it was obvious that he appreciated what we had to offer.

He already had a great team in place, and based on the landscape at the time I was not prepared to fully commit to just one organization. Burt was already in talks with Cage Fury Fighting Championships as well.

It was a productive meeting, but we decided to sit on it and see how things played out. Of course just seven months later I was no longer with the UFC and working with Ray at World Series of Fighting. I always tell cutmen to be prepared during each and every fight because there is no telling what will happen. I guess the same thing can be said about life. Be prepared for anything because you never can know exactly what to expect.

40 OPTIONS

After getting back in action with WS22, I worked a handful more WSOF events. WS29 was at Greeley, Colorado in March 2016. I met with Bruce Deifek, one of the owners of the promotion. He offered me a really nice package to come on board full time with them. He even offered me a percentage of the company.

I really appreciated the offer, but he wanted me to work with them exclusively. Once again, I didn't think I was ready to commit to one organization.

At the same time I'd been talking with Scott Coker once again. Andre Ward was scheduled to fight Sullivan Barrera in Oakland about a week after WS29. The Wednesday before Andre's fight I talked with WSOF CEO, Carlos Silva. He's a great guy, really everyone at WSOF are good people. I told Carlos that I just couldn't commit to one organization. I wanted to work as many shows as I could and I wanted to educate and try to get everybody on the right page. I told him that fighter safety was my number one priority, and I wanted to help as many as I could.

Carlos understood that completely, and even though I didn't take the tremendous offer I still work with WSOF as often as I can.

The following day, the Thursday before Andre's fight, I flew to Oakland and rented a car. I drove to San Jose to meet with Scott and his team. We talked about what I could do for them, and I explained my situation. Scott basically gave me all that I asked for. He said, "Stitch, I understand that you have boxing and they pay a lot more. If we have a show the same day you have boxing, take the boxing. If there's no boxing and we have a show, give us that date. If we don't have a date and there's another show you can work, please take it. If you want sponsors, get sponsors. And if there's any way we can help, we will."

It was a win-win scenario for me, and I couldn't thank Scott enough for it.

My first show under contract with Bellator was in Uncasville, Connecticut at the Mohegan Sun. I'd actually worked Bellator Dynamite in San Jose some seven months earlier. That was a wonderful experience. The show was a co-promotion between Bellator and Glory Kickboxing.

Tito Ortiz fought in the main event against Liam McGeary. Tito lost via an inverted triangle, but it was great to see him fight once again as his career winds down.

It was also great that the show involved Glory Kickboxing. I saw Nobuyuki Sakakibara. He was the co-founder and president of PRIDE, and I'd known him for a long time since I used to work PRIDE events in Japan. I can thank Josh Barnett for those PRIDE days. He brought me over to be his cutman, and he turned out to be a great agent as he set me up for wrapping hands at five hundred bucks a pop.

Anyway, Sakakibara now has Rizin Fighting Federation. The promotion is working to bring back those old PRIDE days. He asked if I'd come to Japan to work Rizin's end of the year shows. I jumped at the opportunity.

I was sitting cageside talking with Lenne Hardt. MMA fans have dubbed her as "The Screaming PRIDE Lady" for her amazing ability to announce fighters with a shrill voice that sounds awesome. Lenne and I have a little connection through the Air Force. She grew up as an Air Force brat, and of course I spent four years in the Air Force.

I felt a tap on my shoulder, and turned around to see a smiling Fedor Emelianenko. We gave each other a big hug and chatted for a moment. I find it interesting that I always run into him at events, and it's always an honor to have such a legend come up to me to say hi.

It was a great start for me working with Bellator. Scott had given me some tickets, so my son, Jacob, came down. He got to meet all the guys and it was great to show him off. I've always been so proud of him.

During the event, I couldn't help but think of where I was just under two months earlier. The Bloody Elbow interview had been released and I got the call from Marc. Now I was sitting in a packed arena talking with Fedor Emelianenko and Lenne Hardt and planning for my next trip to Japan for Rizin. Things were working out.

41 RIZIN

I've been fortunate to do a lot of autograph signings with some outstanding fighters: King Mo, Randy Couture, Royce Gracie, Cung Le, and many others. During the autograph signings they'll often have a contest and whoever wins, I'll wrap their hands.

After the wrap I cut it off so it keeps its form, and then I sign it. It's a pretty cool souvenir for a fight fan.

We were in St. Louis for Bellator's second Dynamite show. We held a signing and they did the contest. A guy won and he stepped up so I could wrap his hand. He was stoked, and there were a lot of people gathered around watching and taking pictures or video.

I finished, and we took pictures with the wrap on his hand. He was smiling from ear to ear. Then as I was cutting it off, I gashed his wrist. I couldn't believe it, and I felt like such an idiot!

When I first started my quest to become a cutman I practiced for hours and hours by wrapping my own hands. One time I cut the wrap off and took a pretty good chunk of skin out of my wrist. I still have the scar to this day.

Well, it was almost the same place where I cut this guy. It was a pretty good cut, and I felt terrible about it. I quickly butterflied it with tape to close it up, but it needed stitches. "Look, man, I'm sorry, but you're going to have to go get stitches," I said.

I told the staff, and unfortunately this guy was freaking out to the point where I was afraid he'd faint. I sat him down and tried to calm him as everyone looked on. I was so embarrassed.

A medical team finally came and took him away to the hospital. Sure enough, he ended up getting some stitches. You know, you're good at what you do, but you're not perfect at what you do. This was definitely a prime example of that.

I apologized to him as I gave him my card. I told him to call me to let me know how he was doing. He never did. Now he's got a hand wrap, and a scar and a story to tell thanks to me messing up.

It happens to the best of us, but I sure did feel bad about it.

I didn't feel so bad a few months before this incident. I was in Japan for Rizin. I thought back to my first time going to Japan for a PRIDE event. The plane bounced along at 35,000 feet for what seemed like an endless stretch of time. The size of the Pacific truly is amazing, and it hadn't gotten any smaller since that first trip across.

Despite the long flight, I was excited to be back in Japan. The people there are such good MMA fans. They know the sport and are extremely polite. *Creed* had just come out in Japan, and so many fans came up to me to tell me how much they liked it and that I did a great job. They made me feel like a million bucks.

It had been a while since I'd been at the Saitama Super Arena. It's a pretty spectacular arena with movable seating so they can host pretty much any event you can think of. I walked through the arena before the fights on December 29 to check the layout and see where I'd be stationed, just basically doing my homework. I was actually there for both events, this one and then part two on New Year's Eve.

It was at the Dynamite event in San Jose when Sakakibara

asked me to work this inaugural Rizin event, and it was also the big announcement that Fedor would come out of retirement to fight once again.

As I walked around the ring I saw Fedor being interviewed. He saw me and stopped the interview. He came over and gave me a big hug. His cameraman was there, and Fedor told him to take a photos of the two of us. He did so, and eventually sent them to me.

As Fedor went back to the interview, I thought that I must be doing something right to have people of this magnitude to go out of their way to give me a hug and say hi. I've always thought that Fedor is the best of the best in MMA, and he's a tremendous person as well. It humbles me when someone like him goes out of his way to say hi.

The event kept me busy with one knockout after another. They hadn't really given me any direction on who to wrap. Muhammed Lawal, "King Mo," wanted me to wrap his hands, but he already had a Japanese guy wrapping it. I was a little hesitant to step in and do it, but after his first fight, a knockout of Brett McDermott, he hurt his hand.

I decided that he needed my support so I wrapped his hand for the rest of the tournament. He went on to win it on New Year's Eve, and he acknowledged me afterward. I really appreciated it.

During part two on New Year's Eve, I worked Bob Sapp's corner as he fought Akebono. These two are absolute legends in Japan. I was working Sapp's corner along with Master Toddy, who was my master when I was training in Thailand in the 70s.

Akebono got cut in the back of the head. He was bleeding like a stuck pig. The promoter's assistant came over to me. "We need you over here."

I went over to help out, and Toddy was yelling, "You're not supposed to go over there!"

He wasn't too happy with me, but he didn't realize that I was there to work with everybody. I wasn't really assigned to work with specific fighters. I haven't had the chance to let him know the situation so I hope he isn't too mad at me!

But man, Akebono bled and bled. I had two towels soaked in his blood when it was all said and done. For a while we kept him in the fight, but the cut was just too bad. Sapp ended up winning the technical decision.

I'd wrapped Fedor's hands a few times before, but I didn't get to on this night. He fought a guy from India named Singh Jaideep, and I guess you could say it was a funny fight. The skill levels were from A to Z. Now I'm not taking anything away from Jaideep. He is willing to get in the ring and fight, but he was up against possibly the greatest fighter of all time.

Fedor settled in for the first minute and then exploded and ended up in the mount. He punched Jaideep until he tapped. It was a good comeback fight for Fedor.

It was New Year's Eve and I was working with my good friend Big John McCarthy. His wife, Elaine, was there as well. After the show I went to his room and we did his podcast. It was almost midnight but there were no fireworks or poppers going off. It was just another day in the office for us, and I wouldn't have it any other way.

42 FIGHTERS FIRST

The events are rolling by as I'm continuing to do what I love. Despite no longer being with the UFC, I'm excited for where I am and the direction of the sport. When Rory MacDonald signed with Bellator he made sure to lock in that I would always be scheduled to wrap his hands. From the time he came up in the UFC as a young kid I'd always wrapped his hands.

Photo: Scott Coker

It's exciting to see what Scott is doing with Bellator. He is signing big fighters and the promotion is growing. Bellator's slogan is "Fighters First," and I wholeheartedly agree with that. It is what I have built my career on. Taking care of the fighters is the top priority for me. All the other stuff is great, but making sure that the fighters get every chance to go back out there for one more round is why I do what I do.

Bellator is in the position that the UFC used to be in. It is much more of a family. It hasn't become so big to the point that you end up having a lot of non-MMA people involved. Scott Coker is fostering this family environment and he wants people to know that he cares about them and they are important to the promotion.

I'm really lucky to be able to work in this atmosphere.

The sport is no doubt headed for many more changes. There will surely be ups and downs, but I can guarantee that I will be involved as long as I can still do my job effectively.

I've truly been blessed throughout my life to have so many wonderful and supportive people around me. I'd like to leave you with a little bit of advice.

When you are presented with an opportunity, don't be afraid to take the risk and go for it. Even if it may seem improbable, or even crazy, believe in yourself. And if you decide to try to achieve something great, understand that it's a process. It might not be easy. As a matter of fact, sometimes it might seem unreachable. Keep going!

You never know where you'll end up. I'm proof, and I've loved every bit of my life, from the fields of Planada, to Madison Square Garden, and beyond.

43 FINAL CHAPTER

As I close out this book, I look back at the wonderful life I was given. "Given" is the proper word to use, because nowhere in my wildest dreams did I ever expect to experience a journey like the one I am on. As one good thing after another happens to me, I often ask myself, "Why was I the chosen one?"

The things that I have done and the great people I have met on this journey are evidence that someone up there is using me as an example. I fully understand and accept the position I was given in life. I now understand what my mission is.

As a young child, we went through hard times, but my brothers and sister and I were always encouraged to think positive. That was the strength that gave us the drive to be who we are today.

Looking back and knowing what I know now, my parents struggled financially and had nothing to offer by way of material things, so they showered us with love and taught us to respect each other and work hard.

I never forget the time on my thirteenth birthday, only four days after Christmas. My mother gave me a newly minted Kennedy 50-cent piece as my birthday gift. She felt bad, and explained that this was all they had to offer. It was not much in value, but it has been a priceless lesson in life. It is not what you give, but how you give it.

Depending on how you approach life, remember that everything has a positive and a negative. The yin and the yang, up and down, left and right, etc. If you let the negative things in life dictate your next move, you will not be able to enjoy the wonderful things that life has to offer. Turn the negative into a positive.

Another example of my parents thinking positive was Halloween when I was ten or eleven. Winter in the San Joaquin Valley is difficult financially because the crops are dormant and there is very little work. Since many families where struggling and not giving candy, my father and mother took me, my brothers Michael and Ernie, and my sister, Belen, to Merced to go Treat or Treating.

We parked and went house to house laughing and filling our bags with candy. We came to this huge house, rung the door bell and yelled, trick or treat. The man asked us where we were from. We proudly said Planada, and with no hesitation, he told us to go back and trick and treat there and closed the door on us. This was my first experience of discrimination.

I saw the anger in my father's eyes, and I knew he wanted to kick his ass. My mother being the positive one, told us that we didn't need his candy anyway and took us to the next house. We continued going house to house, having a great time, and ended up with enough candy to last for two or three weeks.

Lesson learned: it is easier to live with love than it is to show hate.

I'll never forget the words that my friend, Polo Perez, told me when I was with him and other friends hanging out at Chulo's house. He looked at me and said, "You inspire us."

Simple words, coming from a simple man, but as I was driving away, I realized at that moment, that the fact that I inspired them, inspired me. It makes me want to do better not for only myself, but for them as well.

Now that I better understand life and the person I am, it is important for me to thank my wife Charlotte and my children, Carla, Angela, Jacob, and Daniel. There were times when we also struggled, and they kept me grounded and focused.

Also, my parents, Ben and Inez, Tio Miguel and my brothers, Jimmy, Benny, Miguel, and Ernie, and sisters, Dorothy, Linda, and Belen, for making me the person I am today.

Finally, a special thanks to Zac Robinson, friend and author, who had a vision and understood my life. He helped create the stories you read in the first and final chapters of "From the Fields to The Garden l and ll."

"Follow Your Dreams, They Do Come True!"

MEETING STITCH

ZAC ROBINSON

I had the idea to give others the opportunity to tell about meeting Stitch, because through the years so many people have told me about their interactions with him. For me, I saw Stitch briefly at UFC 93 in Dublin, Ireland in January 2009.

The following weekend I was sitting on my couch watching Affliction's second MMA event in Anaheim, California, and I saw Stitch. I thought that he must have so many great stories. I did some research and realized that he had not only great stories to tell, but an amazing life story.

I was just a scrub writer with a soon-to-be-released MMA book. I found an email that I thought was his and gathered up all my courage to send him a message asking if he'd be interested in talking about doing a book.

To my surprise, he responded the following day and asked if I could call. I was freaking out! I told him I would. I paced back and forth in my home office and tried my best to get myself prepared. I called Stitch and he couldn't have been nicer.

During that first conversation he told me, "I'm driving the bus to the top, and anybody who wants can come on board."

I was just some guy who was barely even a writer at the time. I'm located in Germany, and Vitali Klitschko was fighting a few weeks after the call. Stitch asked if I'd meet him in Stuttgart.

Again, nervous as hell, I drove to Stuttgart to meet Stitch for breakfast. He was so positive and friendly, and I felt instantly at ease.

We talked for a couple hours over breakfast, and at one point Wladimir Klitschko walked over. Stitch introduced me and said, "He's going to write my book."

As I shook Wladimir's hand I knew that I'd made the right decision and was so glad I had gone through with contacting Stitch. He told me that others had mentioned doing his book, but I was the first to follow through.

Stitch and I shook hands, and that sealed the deal.

I'm proud to say that we are now good friends, and he is without a doubt one of the most incredible people I've ever met. It's an honor to get to work with him to tell his story.

MARK LAWS

Stitch is the cornerstone to all pro cutmen working today. He set the standard to doing the job correctly and efficiently. He has inspired me and countless others to give our fighter "One more Round," and I'm honored to call him a colleague. I was the first American Cutman asked to join the International Cutman Association, after the honorary President, Jacob Stitch Duran, of course. His life's work has influenced me in huge way.

We've only met casually through the ICA and have always missed each other by hours for the same promotions, but he has always been my go to when I was learning. He's always given me the most honest advice about how to deal with people that we knew, promoters etc...It's a shame we never got to work an event together, but my composure, and my calming effect on fighters comes straight from him.

Like me, he is all about educating and helping further the craft. We both believe you can still learn something every time, no matter how many times you've done it. When the ICA called, and said that they'd heard great things about me, I knew the only other cutman from the U.S. was Jacob, and I was blown away.

I just want to carry on his tradition of passing on knowledge and experiences I've learned. Forever the old School cutmen held their knowledge tight due to either competition or insecurity. But when you are at the top of your game you see how important it is for the next generation to keep the standards high, so that's what I do. I always have cutmen and new guys coming to Tennessee to get one-on-one training and to get that valuable cage time. I'm not threatened they're going to take my spot. They just genuinely want to learn from someone they look up to. I'm blessed and honored to share my love and techniques with them.

It was an honor to meet Stitch, believe me. Anyone who knows Stitch knows how humble he is, but his confidence is something else. He is never self-doubting, never afraid to tell you the truth, and always on his A+ game. A lot try to imitate, but very few have that confidence of knowing they control the chaos. It's a beautiful feeling.

Thank you for the opportunity to show love to the man that molded me. There isn't any greater honor.

JOSH HISER

What started out as a normal UFC weekend in Manchester, England, turned out to be the best guys-out weekend of my life. I was fortunate enough to meet and hang out with Stitch. When I met him he immediately treated me like we had known each other for years.

I remember going to dinner that Friday and just listening to story after story and being mesmerized by the things he has done. It didn't stop there, though. On Saturday after the fights he invited us back to the after party and treated us like we were the celebrities.

The best part of the weekend though was definitely getting to have the knockout wrap put on my hand by the man himself. He was getting interviewed and photographer, Martin McNeill, the one who took the famous bloody Joe Stevenson shot, took photos of Stitch wrapping my hand for me. It was a once-in-a-lifetime experience.

Stitch is the guy that will go out of his way to make a fan happy. However, when you meet him he doesn't treat you like a fan, he treats you like a friend.

KURT DANIELS

I first met Stitch at the UFC Boston Expo. It was August 2010. I had competed in a No Gi Competition earlier in the morning. I placed in the tournament, so I had still had my medal proudly hung around my neck when I headed to the booths to meet the UFC fighters and the vendors. I saw Stitch at one of the booths and thought I'd stop in to get an autograph.

I got so much more.

Stitch noticed my medal and said, "Oh nice, a fighter."

At the time I didn't think of myself as a fighter. Stitch continued to talk to me and build my confidence as he called me, "A Warrior."

I snapped a picture with him and went along.

Later, I decided after I printed the picture I would try to send it to Stitch to see if he would sign it for me. When I tracked down an e-mail address for him, he quickly responded with his home address and a yes to signing and sending me back the picture of the two of us. Years later, as I loosely stayed in touch with him I traveled to Las Vegas to prepare for a fight. I reached out to him ahead of time to see if we could meet up for lunch while I was in town.

He again responded with a yes. So one day after training with

Ryan Couture, Ryan and I headed to have lunch with Stitch. We sat there in awe listening to Stitch tell stories of his UFC days and fighters.

As we talked I mentioned that next time I was in Vegas to fight I would want him in my corner as my cutman. He again quickly said sure.

We said our goodbyes, snapped another picture, and headed to our cars. As we walked I said, "I'll let you know when the fight happens here."

His response was priceless to me. "I'm part of the team, right?"

To that I said, "Yes you are, yes you are."

That is my meeting of Stitch and why I hold the man in high regard. He is a very giving humble man, with a lot of life experiences.

STEFAN SCHOTT

I had thought about getting the knowledge of a cutman for quite a while, but never knew one who could teach me.

I found Stitch on Facebook, but never thought it was the real Stitch. I sent him a pm and asked if he would give cutman seminars.

He replied and told me that he would go to Munich (I live in Germany) for the Klitschko vs. Chisora fight in a few weeks and that we could figure something out. I headed down to Munich and didn't know what to expect. I met Stitch in the hotel where he introduced me to guys like Michael Buffer and the whole team Klitschko. It was like I was a part of the family as well.

We had a cool evening at the hotel bar and I felt very welcoming. The next day he invited me for breakfast, and during the day he showed me everything I needed to know to begin my path as a cutman.

Cherry on top—he managed to bring me to the Klitschko fight in the evening with a ringside seat.

I had an awesome weekend and I am proud to call myself Stitch's first student from Germany.

It was the beginning of a good friendship and I recognized

that there is a reason why all the fighters want Stitch in their corner. He has such a positive attitude and is so down to earth. Whenever I meet him in the states or here in Germany I have a great time hanging around with this vato!

MICHAEL SCHMIDT

How I met your mother…Sorry, how I met Stitch! My name is Michael Schmidt, I was born in 1969 in Gelsenkirchen, Germany.

I was an eager fan of Mohammed Ali. When I became older, I tried to become a boxer, but unfortunately without any talent!

My coach at that time, the former German Champion in welterweight and number two European champion Michael Kopzog said I had character, but zero talent. I also started the sport to late. I became a plumber, and then a physical therapist.

In my education I got to know Sascha Wietzorreck, an MMA fighter and coach in Germany. He gave a course in self-defense in our state health school. At that time I suffered from tinnitus. The constant peeps in the ear brought me almost to insanity.

Sascha wanted to demonstrate a rear naked choke. It cracked immensely in my cervical vertebra column and suddenly my ear noise was gone. He had cured me! Sounds funny, for me it was like heaven. In the deepest gratitude I served him from now on as a responsible person in his MMA team as a physical therapist.

I had no notion what a cutman was. I concentrated more upon the fighter than around the guys with the cotton bud in the hand.

Later, at a tournament called "Kiru," Jörg "Marshmallow"

Lothmann, a German MMA and BJJ legend, shouted to me, "Hey, cutman, stick this guy together here."

I'd seen cutmen work, but often what they did didn't correspond with what I'd learned regarding hygiene. I found some fights and videos with Stitch. I recognized immediately that he is an absolute full professional.

He worked cleanly, fast, and completely properly. This had impressed me immediately. I can still remember well my first attempts to wrap a hand. My God they were shit! Unfortunately, there was nobody who taught me the right way. Some tried, but their wraps were not better than mine, and some of the wraps were probably unlawful.

I put together all my courage and tried to contact Jacob. The first contacts were by email, and then by Facebook or phone. He answered my questions and helped me so well. It completely made no difference where he was or with whom he sat at the table, I could always count on him.

I did not know the German cutmen at all, experienced men like Walter Knieps, Dominik Junge, or Oliver Schröder. That's why I worked 99% for MMA and not for boxing. After I brought out my book, I heard from them. Some weren't happy about the book, but unfortunately nobody wrote a cutman book at the German market. If they had written a book, I would have bought it.

Stitch didn't keep the trade a secret. Work together, not against each other (this is my saying).

When Francesco Pianeta fought Klitschko, we planned a breakfast with my good friend Stefan Schott with whom I have started here in Germany as one of the first pioneers of MMA cutmen.

If I am honest, I could not sleep the night before. I was so nervous before the first personal meeting in Heidelberg. When I fetched Stefan in Mainz, he drove so I could sleep another two hours before we met our hero, Stitch.

When we came in this great hotel, the doorkeeper welcomed us and opened the door, a very nice hotel with five-stars in the middle of Heidelberg. We announced ourselves and took a seat in the lobby to wait.

Exactly on time, Stitch walked down the stairs and smiled at Stefan (they had already met). I was really nervous. Stitch welcomed us and invited us for the breakfast. We sat with the Klitschko Team, Michael Buffer, and the management of the Klitschkos. This was a unique feeling.

After some small talk and a breakfast of roasted pancakes, with bacon, onions, and chili, there was one more interview with him, which I had planned for my book.

When we finished, it was clear to me that this day will always remain in my memory.

At the time Stitch wasn't a member of the ICA, but in 2014 we organized a world championship for cutmen. Cutmen from around the world came to Cologne to see who the world's best hand wrapper was.

It was a real competition, but the main idea was to meet each other. Adam Gigli from Norfolk, England won. Second was our president, Federico Catizone, from Italy, and third was Tommy McCormack from Dublin, Ireland.

It was a historical moment, because Stitch gave us the honor and spent a miraculous week with us, we carried out seminars and exchanged our knowledge, a great community of cutmen from the whole world.

The presenter of this event, Peter Schmithuisen, front man of the German MMA Supporters, forgot the money for his official t-shirts. Who paid-up for the bill?

Stitch!

When we cleaned up the area, he helped like any other member. You can talk for hours about all possible subjects with him, from spiritual nature or all other stuff. It was like he is one of us. And he is, but he is seen as a legend.

I had never met a person who carries this fame, but still is so natural and honest. He is self-sacrificing with a measure of empathy that is impressive. I feel blessed and honored I can call him a personal friend.

Even if many will smile at this, I love this person, exactly like Vitali Klitschko, who said to him, "Stitch, I am not gay, but I love you."

If God may protect him and his miraculous family and give still many, many years, which we will hopefully, spend together. There is no cutman in the whole world with this aura, this heart, and this mind, Stitch is the number one, amen! Your dear friend, Michael Schmidt, AKA Cutman Liberty.

PACO ESTRADA

It was back in 2006 at the Mandalay Bay in Las Vegas when I met Jacob "Stitch" Duran. We were on set, filming the movie, *Rocky Balboa*. I was playing a high-roller boxing fan. Stitch was playing the cutman/cornerman for Mason Dixon, played by Antonio Tarver.

There was a lot of down time between takes, and I recognized Stitch from the boxing and MMA scene and was hoping I could meet him. During the six days of filming, I was lucky enough to meet Stitch and realized he was the most genuine and down-to-earth celebrity I have ever met.

Stitch had a disposable camera on set and I told him that I could develop the film for him. Stitch took me up on my offer and I developed some great pictures as we developed a great friendship.

We kept in touch and have gotten to know each other's families. I was lucky enough to be Stitch's Assistant-Cutman for UFC 58 USA vs. Canada for the epic fight between George St. Pierre and BJ Penn. I was amazed by Stitch's presence behind the scenes, as he wrapped the fighters' hands and talked to everyone. He was like the Mayor of UFC.

Stitch always gave my two boys and myself the VIP treatment during all the weigh-ins in Las Vegas and continues to be more than a great friend, but more like family.

MICHELLE IRWIN

I used to work in Germany for the U.S. Military and was involved in an MMA tour. A group of fighters and their cutman came to visit with the Soldiers in our area. I had no idea what to expect.

I had heard several people talking about Jacob "Stitch" Duran.

"I love to watch him wrap a hand and tell a story to young fighters. It is inspiring," one person told me.

"Don't you know who he is? He's famous in the UFC/MMA world," stated another.

Honestly, I had no idea "who" he was, but I was honored to be included in the whirlwind tour. Anticipation was overshadowed by the busyness of preparation.

Upon first meeting Stitch, I was tired and merely doing my job. He was one of four distinguished guests visiting the Soldiers in our Garrison that week. Initially, I had no impression of Stitch. However, that changed quickly as I spent the next four days riding alongside him to every event, speaking engagement, and dinner that was scheduled.

Stitch cut through the formalities right away. He barely indulged in conversations about his life without making certain that his story taught me something about me and my life. I realized that Stitch was genuinely more interested in knowing me and learning about my life than he was about impressing me with stories of his. Just being in his presence for those four days gave me peace as I struggled with turmoil in my life. Our conversations gave me insight and his directness cut through all of my excuses and gave me direction.

Meeting Stitch was more than I could have ever expected, and now I know why so many fighters want him in their corner.

STITCH'S TOP LISTS

Top Five Favorite Fights

1. Wanderlei Silva/Chuck Liddell
2. Shogun Rua/Dan Henderson
3. Robby Lawler/Rory McDonald
4. Gilbert Melendez/Diego Sanchez
5. Nate Diaz/Conner McGregor 1

Top Five Worst Cuts

1. Marvin Eastman vs. Vitor Belfort
2. Jay Hieron vs. Jonathan Goulet
3. Robbie Lawler vs. Rory MacDonald
4. Brock Lesnar vs. Cain Velasquez
5. Evan Tanner vs. David Loiseau

Top Three Scariest Knockouts

1. CroCop vs. Gabriel Gonzaga
2. Michael Bisping vs. Dan Henderson
3. Edson Barboza vs. Terry Etim

Top Three Fighters You'd Want on Your Side in a Street Fight

1. Nick Diaz
2. Nate Diaz
3. Wanderlei Silva

Top Three Funniest Fighters

1. Marcus Davis
2. Cole Escovedo
3. Pat Barry

Top Three Favorite Fight Venues

1. Mandalay Bay
2. Arena at Montreal
3. Arena at Rio

Top Five Favorite Cities

1. Rio
2. Tokyo
3. Las Vegas
4. Montreal
5. New York

Top Three Tips for Long Flights

1. Plenty of water
2. Rest
3. Plenty of water

Top Three Favorite Musicians

1. Santana
2. Little Joe y La Familia
3. WAR

Top Three Favorite Sports Movies

1. *Creed*, of course
2. *Major League*
3. *Rocky*

Top Three Favorite Movies

1. *Jurassic Park*
2. *Shawshank Redemption*
3. *Lone Survivor*

Top Three Favorite Sports Teams

1. Yankees
2. Raiders
3. University of Miami

ABOUT THE AUTHORS

STITCH DURAN is regarded as the best cutman in the business. You can connect with Stitch online through Facebook and Twitter. This is his second book.

ZAC ROBINSON is the author of many MMA and baseball books. You can find Zac on Facebook, Twitter, and Amazon.

To schedule an event with the authors contact:
Stitchpremium@gmail.com

www.ingramcontent.com/pod-product-compliance
Lightning Source LLC
Chambersburg PA
CBHW071527040426
42452CB00008B/917